The Rh␣
Ou␣
Valley

By Brian Pattimore

Introduction

Hello I am Brian I come from a strong mining background from the Rhondda Valley with my Father Thomas John Pattimore working in Dinas Mine and four other mines my Uncles Davey Pattimore, Tommy Martin, Dick Jones all worked in the mines along with other members of my family. As a child I spent many holidays in the Rhondda and at Porthcawl and in present days I still visit the Rhondda. I still have family throughout the Rhondda Valley I am married with four Daughters and Eleven Grandchildren at present I live in Southampton. In this book I would like to share a bit of History of the Rhondda Valley along with a selection of my poems of Wales and mining. I am a foster carer and look after learning disabilities children

I dedicate this book to all Miners and their families

Thanks To
Ruth my wife for supporting me in the writing of this book.
Sarah Phillips my Niece for giving me the inspiration to write this book.
South Wales police museum for their cooperation in the writing of this book.

As I lay and dream of the Rhondda how it could have been
Mountains grey with dust rail tracks gaining rust
Then the pits began to close and the Rhondda began to grow
Work became short mining was all we were thought
Men traveled far and wide trying to hide the hurt inside
Some remained on the dole destroying their pride and soul
Some moved away to earn their pay wishing they could stay
Government made the choice not listening to the Rhondda voice   The hurt would last forever more as the mines closed their doors   Now the Rhondda green and bright but let's not forget the miners fight They fought for work and pay but no attention did the government pay   A new community began to grow now men no longer went below   Will the Rhondda fully recover only time will discover   The Rhondda will remain in our hearts a community no one can part

Trehafod

If you look up the 1847 tithe map of the area it will shows a number of farms on the area that was to become Trehafod, these farms were named, Hafod Uchaf, Hafod Ganol and Hafod Fawr. It is reported Trehford was to take its name these farms. *Hafod* is a welsh word that can mean "summer dwelling" or "upland farm".

The railway station of trehaford lies on the main Rhondda line

The River Rhondda the railway line and river border the village on either side.

Trehafod is now most famous for the Rhondda Heritage Park which was once the Lewis Merthyr colliery, (my Father worked at Lewis Merthyr at the age of 14) at the peak time for coal mining production, one of the most productive collieries in the .south wales Cole industry

Because of the position of the river flowing very close to a lot of houses within the village there have been a number of flooding's. The biggest floods were in 1960, which claimed the life of one man who lived in Afon Street. *Afon* means river in the welsh language in most streets, the whole lower level of buildings was submerged by water. Other years that flooding's have occurred were 1921, 1929, 1979 and most recently in the mid-1990s. In the late 1990s the Trehafod stretch of the Rhondda riverbank was reinforced, in an effort to prevent future flooding's.

During Queen Elizabeth ll Jubilee tour of the UK Trehaford was visited on 13th June 2002

Other royal guests who have visited in the past 1912 King George V and Queen Mary made a visit

The station at Trehafod was opened on 4 February 1861, and was originally named *Havod*. The Welsh spelling *Hafod* was adopted in November 1890, and altered to *Trehafod* on 1 January 1905.

The 18th July 1889 Barry Railway

Opened their main line between Hafod Junction and their new Docks which was situated in Barry and immediately began carrying coal and passenger trains until 16th March 1896, the new service running which was Porth and Barry via Hafod and the Barry Railway's newly opened station at Pontypridd

Passenger services along the Barry route were diverted via the former Taff Vale station in Pontypridd from 10th July 1930, but coal trains to Barry Docks continued to use the ex-Barry Railway route until June 1951 when they were diverted via radyr Services at this station are

Monday-Saturday, there is a half-hourly daytime service to Cardiff Central southbound and to Treherbert northbound, dropping to hourly in the evening. There is a two-hourly service in each direction on Sundays.

The Heritage Centre once Lewis Merthyr

Was It Worth It

Was it worth it all those years ago?
My answer my friend is I don't know
Father and Sons in the dark a mile below
All in search of the black coal
Bodies dark and scared
My father and his Brother worked so hard
The mines now all have gone
The sirens all gone that sounded so long
Once again the Valley is a beautiful green
Sadly for my father it's too late to be seen
For the dust has done its job
All my father did was his job
Was it worth it I don't know?
For down the mines I did not go

Porth

Industrial growth

It was in 1809, the first coal pit in the Rhondda to be sunk, further up the valley in

Dinas but a lack of a transportation network impacted greatly on the profitability of mining Cole as an industry in the region. This problem was tackled by constructing a one mile tramline which connected mines in Dinas to a tramline built by Richard Griffith at Denia Pontypridd), which linked to a private canal work that joined the Canal at Treforest Coffins tramline followed the southern bank of the River Rhondda and ran through Porth.

The existence of the tramline made the development of the Porth and Cymmer region far more attractive, and by the middle of the 19th century there was an impetus to expand coal mining in the area. In 1841 Richard Lewis joined Coffin in trying to exploit the region with his level built at Cymmer. This resulted in the construction of around fifty miner's cottages, several of which were located in Porth. In 1844 Lewis Edwards who came from Newport and George Gethin who came from penygrieg opened a small level at Nyth-bran on the eastern borders of Porth, the village's first coal mine. This was followed in 1845 by the sinking of the Porth Colliery by David James who came from Merther the success of which saw him build the Llwyncelyn Colliery in 1951, also in Porth. It was by 1850 that the Taff Railway had been extended to Cymmer replacing the tramline, allowing direct access between the lower Rhondda and the ports of Cardiff.

In 1850 the Troedyrhiw Colliery (later to become the Aber-Rhondda Colliery), which was sunk on the northern borders of Porth and the neighboring village of Ynyshir by Leonard Hadley of Caerleon five years earlier, came into the ownership of a new consortium known as the Troedyrhiw Coal Company. James Thomas, a former miner, Matthew Cop, a Cardiff docks man and John Lewis, a grocer from Aberdare, formed this company. In 1852 the same company opened the Tynewydd Colliery at the junction of the Rhondda Fawr and Fach rivers, Porth's fourth mine. The mine quickly struck the Rhondda No. 3 seam, and coking ovens were built at the surface providing further employment.

With the increase in population, transport links began to improve in the Rhondda. This was hampered by subsidence caused by the mining underground, which resulted in the roads of Porth Square sinking by eight foot. In 1860 a two horsed omnibus service was introduced between Porth and

Pontypridd but was replaced by a system of horse drawn tramcars in 1888. Although the tramline and subsequently the railway had passed through Porth for two decades, servicing the collieries, it was not until 1861 that the village had its first railway station; and a passenger service did not commence until January 1863.

As the population continued to increase, businesses and infrastructure grew around the coal industry. The Rhondda Urban Council chose Porth as one of two sites to build gas works and the area around Porth Square and Hannah Street became the commercial center of the village. One of the more notable businesses to open in Porth was the Thomas & Evans grocer one of the first of a chain of shops owned by William Thomas and William Evans two entrepreneurs from Pembrokeshire. Evans became an important figure in the growth of Porth, and in the late 1890s he opened a jam factory and the Welsh Hills Mineral Water factory, later to become Corona carbonated drinks, which would remain a major manufacturer within the village up until the 1980s.

Coal mining in the Rhondda continued to expand throughout the early 20th century, although no further mines were sunk in Porth. The population continued to grow but conditions became hard after the Great Depression, and by the mid-1920s unemployment among mine workers rocketed. Matters worsened after the general strike which was to be disastrous which saw many miners out of work for months. As mechanization allowed other mining areas to become more profitable, the antiquated Rhondda mines sunk nearly 75 years earlier were unable to modernize and one-by-one began to close. Porth, like the rest of the Rhondda, was built solely around the coal industry, and with its collapse came mass unemployment, resulting in economic migration. There was a brief respite during the Second World War, when employment rose sharply. This was partially due for a need for Rhondda steam coal, but also due to large munition factories built in Bridgend, Hirwaun and Treforest (My Mother worked in the Treforest factory) to which the workers commuted. With the end of the war it was apparent that unemployment would return, but to ensure that the newly found factory skills gained during the previous six years were lost the British Government passed the Distribution of Industry Act in 1945. This saw 25 new industries come to the Rhondda, six of them based in Porth. They ranged from Messrs. Jacob Beatus' box making company, a metal toy factory and a branch of Remploy aimed at disabled workers.

Early history

History shows that in prehistoric times the area now known as Porth was uninhabited wooded area. Although there is evidence of settlements in the upper reaches of the valley, only Cairns used as way-markers have been discovered on the higher points in the Porth area. It was during the medieval period the area came under the commote of Glynrhondda within the center of penychen, though the area was still uninhabited. Although there were no permanent buildings of note at this time, it is known that the area would have experienced travelers. Who built two bridges over the River Rhondda at Porth, the Pont Rheola and Pont y Cymmer? Both bridges date back to at least the 1530s when they were reference made by antiquary John Leland. These bridges were wooden in construct and were later to be rebuilt in stone. The first buildings of note in the region were built to the south of Porth in the community known today as Cymmer, this consisted mainly of a chapel, Capel y Cymmer (1743) and a mill on the south bank of the River Rhondda. It was by the 18th century there were a handful of farmhouses, mainly in the northern slopes of Llwyncelyn. During this pre-industrial era, the locale was known as Cymmer, an old Welsh word that describes the point where two rivers converge. It was only during the industrial period that the mining operations of the Porth Estate and the subsequently named railway station that saw the name Porth adopted.

A Miners Prayer

Please God keep me safe
In this dark and dusty place
If my time should come
My work in this mine done
Please send an Angel to show me the way
For how to get to Heaven I don't know the way
I know I must go to the light
Which will take me out of this dark grey night
If I have to come back home
Please let my family know I'm not alone
So please God keep me safe today
I will gladly meet you another day

Rhondda Fawr

Trealaw

Trealaw is a dormitory town of the more famous
Tonypandy, its name translates from the welsh language as
'the Town of Alaw', which derives from Alaw Goch or Alaw
Coch (red melody), the bardic name of David (Dafydd)
Williams (d. 1863) the father of Judge Gwilym Williams

11

(1839–1906), who founded the village (along with that of Williamstown, a village to the south of Trealaw) during the 'coal-rush' of the 19th century. Judge Williams is also commemorated in Trealaw by Judges Hall (in full, the Judge Gwilym Williams Memorial Hall) and in Ynyscynon Road, named after the Williams' family seat at Ynyscynon, near Aberdare in the Cynon Valley. Judges Hall is a community venue used in its heyday for Variety performances, boxing tournaments and snooker. Today it is used for Bingo and youth activities.

Although Trealaw is considered to date from the 1860/70s, it does have an earlier history. On the river bank, near the confluence of Nant Clydach with the Rhondda Fawr River, stood Ynys-y-Crug, a 12th-century timber motte and bailey castle. Until recent years, a mound about 12 feet high by 100 feet in length remained, which over the centuries had acquired the name of Gibbet Hill, indicating perhaps, that in the area's medieval period, it was a place of execution. However, latterly, development of the mid-Rhondda by-pass road has removed all traces of the castle.

Trealaw is the site of one of the Rhondda's largest cemeteries, Llethrddu (Black slope), which opened in 1875. In the cemetery are many reminders of the tragic loss of life which was an everyday reality during the valley's coal mining era, including most of the thirty-one victims of the Rhondda's last mining disaster at the Cambrian Colliery in May 1965.

Because of its position, it is served by three railway stations; Dinas, Tonypandy and Llwynypia. Various bus routes are also provided across South Wales.

In addition to the traditional terraces, several modern housing developments have been constructed in Trealaw. Foundry Road also has a number of industrial units.

There are two local primary schools in the immediate area; Alaw Primary School and Trealaw Junior School. Children who live near the Tonypandy end of the village are more likely to attend Tonypandy Community College; and children who live near Porth are more likely to attend Porth County Community School.

Trealaw has one of the largest cemeteries

From Lad To Man

In the Valleys I was born
A Miner to be I was sworn
At the age of fourteen
I lost my childhood to the coal seams
Ffaldau Colliery Area 2
Lamp check number 645
Will this be my last day a live? From Lad to Man
Will this be my last day a live?
I pick up my lamp and tools off the bar
Already this mine has left it scar
In the cage we would go
To take us that mile below
Is there gas in this tunnel below?
My Carney would let me know
There's no sweeter sound than his song
In these tunnels miles long

My Fathers Lamp checks

Penygraig

Penygraig (Head of the Rock) is a village and community in the Rhondda Valley in the county borough of Rhondda Cynon Taf, within the boundaries which is glamorgan, Wales. As a community Penygraig contains the neighboring districts known as Dinas Edmondstown Penrhiwfer and Williamstown.

The original settlement which in now Penygraig was called Ffrwd Amos, though as with the rest of the Rhondda before industrialisation the only settlements were farmsteads. In 1832, saw, one of the first Baptist chapels in the Rhondda was built at Penygraig by preacher David Williams.

Industrial Penygraig

When coal mining began in Penygraig in 1857 when Thomas Ellis sank a drift mine. In 1858 Moses Rowlands and Richard Jenkins discovered a seam at Penygraig and would later form the Penygraig Coal Company. The Company sank the first deep pit in the village, The Penygraig Colliery; after which the village would be named. After the Penygraig Colliery showed a successful profit the Naval Colliery Company opened a second deep pit, The Pandy, which reached the steam coal seam in 1879. The Pandy was then sold to the New Naval Colliery Company after three disasters, which then opened three more deep mines The Ely, the Nantgwyn and the Anthony Pits. The New Naval Company would then become part of the Cambrian Combine, owned by the then. The viscount

16

Rhondda the Ely Colliery would be the center of the Cambrian dispute, which in turn would lead to unrest and the Tonypandy Riots

The Naval Colliery pit disasters the first being in 1875

The first of three disasters to occur at the Naval Colliery happened on 4 December 1875 when a flood broke through into the mine, resulting in two miners drowning and the lives of many others placed at risk. Then on 10 December 1880 a gas explosion took the lives of 101 miners out of the 106 who were working in the mine at the time. This was followed on 27 January 1884 when another explosion led to the death of fourteen men. These disasters are likely factors in the Naval Colliery Company selling the mine in 1887.

Dinas

Dinas is a Village close to
Tonypandy in the part of the Borough of Rhondda
Cynon Taf, Wales. Other neighboring settlements are
Penygreig, Trelaw, Cymmer and porth. The word *Dinas* in
modern welsh means "city", but here (as in Old and modern
welsh more generally) it means "hill fort".

Dinas is the site of Dinas Lower Colliery, a mine
sunk by Walter Coffin in 1812 as the first deep coal mine in
the Rhondda valley. This was later followed by the sinking
of the Dinas Middle Colliery in 1832 along the southern
banks of the river Rhondda Fawr, from here coal was
carried by trams via Porth, Cymmer, and Trehaford to
Pontypridd, where it was conveyed by canal to Cardiff. By
1893 production had ceased in both collieries.

In 1841 the 4-mile long Rhondda branch line of the
Taff Vale Railway was opened between Pontypridd and
Dinas, eventually to be extended as far as Treherbert by
1856. Dinas was also home to the first Methodist Chapel
established in the Rhondda, the Ebenezer having been built
around 1830.

The village of Dinas has a very special place in any
history of the Rhondda for it is here that the birth of the coal
industry in the valley, and hence the birth of industrial
Rhondda itself, can truly be said to have taken place. This
development began when Walter Coffin, a businessman
from Bridgend, bought Dinas farm in the early 1800's,
followed subsequently by the mineral rights to Gwaun Ddu
and Gwaun Adda Farms, with the intention of prospecting
the area for coal. The early days of mining in Dinas were

beset by problems as the science of geology was at that time in its infancy, and the extent of the coal measures on the land unproved. Also the Rhondda at that time was bereft of manpower with experience of the mining industry, meaning skilled labor had to be imported and housed in the area.

Additionally at the beginning of the venture Dr.Griffith's tram road terminated three miles below Dinas, making the transportation of any coal produced extremely problematical. However Coffin eventually overcame these problems and by 1841 the Dinas pits owned by Coffin employed 301 men and 113 boys, making them the largest colliery not connected to an ironworks in North Glamorgan.

Dinas Colliery

My Lamp

I pick up my lamp and tools off the bar
Already this mine has left it scar
In the cage we would go
To take us that mile below
Is there gas in this tunnel below?
My Carney would let me know
There's no sweeter sound than his song
In these tunnels miles long

Tonypandy

Pre-industrial history

The Tonypandy area contains several sites, the main one being Mynydd y Gelli. Located to the north-west of the town, the remains of an Iron Age settlement Hen Dre'r Gelli lies on the slopes of Mynydd Y Gelli hill between Tonypandy and Gelli Near the same location are several Bronze Age Cairns

Tonypandy is also the site of one of the only two permanent middle Ages fortifications found within the Rhondda Valley. Named Ynysygrug, it was a lesser motte and bailey earthwork defense. The fortification appears to have consisted of a wooden tower surrounded by a small fortified courtyard. Placed around the 12th or early 13th century, the remains of the fortification were mostly destroyed when the town's railway was constructed in the 19th century. Over the past two hundred years, the fortification had been wrongly thought to be the burial place of Rhys ap Tewdwr or a druidic worship site.

The regional library service recounts that the name 'Tonypandy' means *the meadow of the fulling mill* which was established there in 1838. "E. D. Lewis in his work *The Rhondda Valleys* provides us with an outline history of the mill that once stood in Tonypandy, and from which the town took its name".

Industrial era

In the mid-19th century, the Rhondda began its industrial transformation after the successful excavation of coal. With the extension of the Taff Vale Railway to Treherbert and Maerdy in 1856, the Rhondda grew as absentee Landlords switched their interests from farming to mining. Tonypandy, unlike the surrounding villages, grew as a financial and social hub, providing services and amenities for the neighboring communities.

Pen Pych

To climb Pen Pych if I can
Hope the weather don't spoil my plans
It's been many years since I was last there
If I reach my goal views of the Rhondda I will share
Looking down on the Valley below
Where As a child I used to go
Harcoombe Road is where I'd stay
With Aunty Mary and Uncle Davey
So when I reach my goal
I'll view the memories below
To climb Pen Pych if I can
Please weather don't spoil my plans

Clydach Vale

Before the coming of industrialisation, Clydach Vale was a sparsely populated area. Records show that in the seventeenth century the area was named Dyffryn Clydach (Clydach Vale), and was divided into two areas, Cwmclydach and Blaenclydach. Those two localities are today very much integrated. The Cwmclydach Community Partnership is made up of groups from both villages (and the wider community), plus the Clydach Vale Countryside Park and Mountain Forestry.

In the 1840s mining began in the valley, but this was on a small scale and no pits were sunk at this time. Towards the end of the century there was a marked increase in mining activity, several collieries being opened, including Lefel-Y-Bush (1863), Blaenclydach (1863), Cwmclydach (1864) and Clydach Vale Collieries Nos. 1, 2 and 3.

Industrial conflict

The Clydach Vale collieries would later become synonymous with worker activism within South Wales. Opened in 1872, the Clydach Vale colliery No. 1 was originally sunk by Osbourne Riches and Samuel Thomas and, by 1894, was served by the Taff Vale Railway. Following the death of Thomas in 1879, his sons became managing partners and, in 1895, formed Cambrian Collieries Ltd.

Colliery disasters

On 10 March 1905, an explosion occurred at the Cambrian Colliery No.1. The explosion was heard for miles around the valleys and resulted in the loss of 33 lives and serious injury to 14 others. The accident happened between the day and night shifts, otherwise the death toll would have been far higher.

On 25 November 1941, seven men were killed and 53 were injured when a trolley transporting miners down a sharply sloping shaft ran out of control. The incident happened at the 'Gorky' drift mine, with ninety men and boys taking the spake, an open-sided trolley fitted with cross planks for seating and a central overhead handrail as a holding point, down to the workings 525 yards below. The surface engineman suffered a temporary blackout and the manual brake was disengaged, causing the spake to quickly build up speed. Most of the injuries and fatalities were to miners who leapt from the spake and were thrown back under the trolley due to the narrowness of the drift shaft.

On 17 May 1965, a third major accident occurred at the Cambrian Colliery. An explosion caused by firedamp, after poor ventilation allowed a build-up of flammable gas, killed 31 miners. The ignition point was later identified as an electric arc on an open switch-panel which was being worked on. This was the last major mining disaster in South Wales history.

1910 flood disaster

At about 4.00 p.m. on Friday 11 March 1910, the lives of one adult and five children were lost when pent-up water from an abandoned coalmine burst through into the village.

The mountainside seemed to give way, 'as though from a volcanic eruption' and a torrent of water together with huge amounts of earth, boulders and other debris swept down the hillside. Directly in the path of this torrent lay

Adams Terrace and, according to contemporary newspaper reports, the first house it encountered 'was in a moment completely wrecked like a pack of cards' and its occupants and a ten-week-old baby girl perished.

A three-week-old baby boy also died. The newspaper went on to state that, 'Altogether eleven houses and a shoemaker's shop were wrecked, one being completely washed away'.

Rushing down to the valley floor, the torrent inundated the Clydach Vale School and trapped hundreds of children. Fortunately the time coincided with the homecoming of many miners at the ending of a shift and an immediate rescue effort by them and the school's staff saved all but three of over 950 children. In particular, the headmaster displayed extraordinary bravery in battling the flood and saving many children, for which he was later awarded the Albert Medal.

A brass wall plaque was placed in the school in recognition of the discipline and heroism of the staff in organizing the rescue. In preparation for the 2010 centenary of the disaster, another plaque, with names of the dead, was installed at the school together with a montage of photographs showing the aftermath of the flood.

Cambrian colliery

My Rhondda

My Rhondda where I live
With mountains high and Valleys low
And sometimes it even snows
My Rhondda where I live
With its mountains in different shades of green
Not so long a go
They were covered in coal from below
My Rhondda where I live
With its rivers and its steams
Trickling out from the coal seams
My Rhondda where I live
Was a different colour so they say?
When they called it Rhondda grey

My Rhondda where I live
Is now a Beautiful place?
But it still bears the scars of the pit face

Llwynpia

Llwynypia is a village and community in the Rhondda near Tonypandy in the Rhondda Valley. Before 1850 it was mostly a rural farming area, Llwynypia started to experience a population boom between 1860 and 1920 when the sinking of several coal mines after the discovery of large coal deposits throughout the Rhondda Valleys.

.

Situated on the River Rhondda Fawr where the river changes direction from south-east to southerly, Llwynypia holds evidence of human habitation of Llwynpia from as early as the Bronage age through to modern times. On a hill overlooking the area to the west known as Mynydd Gelli, lies the Iron Age settlement of Hen Dre'r Gelli, a site which also has several Bronze Age cairns

It was not till 1850 when the first mine was sunk in the upper Rhondda in Treherbert but it was not until 1859 that, the first attempt to prospect the area for coal when a small level beneath Llwynypia Farm. This encountered numerous problems, and it was abandoned but in 1862 land leased at Llwynypia and sank the Llwynypia No. 1 pit in 1863. Although facing many difficulties at the No. 1 pit, they continued to endeavor and by 1873 had sunk 4 more pits, now under the name of the Glamorgan Coal Company. The mines became known as the 'Scotch mines', a number of miners went to live and work in Llwynypia. After the owners death in 1902, many tributes was received from the workforce, and in 1906 a statue of the owner was unveiled by a Rhondda MP outside the Llwynypia Miners institute. Much of the cost of the statue was met by donations from the miners of these pits.

In 1908 the Glamorgan Colliery became part of the Cambrian Combine Company. This sparking riots in Tonypandy

The very high quality of Rhondda coal was recognized by the Admiralty which specified it as the fuel of choice for the steam ships of the Royal Navy from the late 19th century. The Llwynypia pits were extracting excellent coking coals and, by the time of World War 1 the village housed around 140 coke ovens. By-products of the coke distillation process was used to light the mines and the narrow streets of miners' cottages known as "terraces". Some of the terraces have been widened but others remain so narrow that a single car can barely pass through.

On 25 January 1932, a gas explosion occurred at the colliery. Eleven workers were killed in the incident, two of whom were members of the rescue party. All perished after inhaling afterdamp following the explosion.

By 1936, of the original six pits opened at the Glamorgan, two remained in operation, employing only 560 workers, as against 2904 employed in 1923. The colliery was eventually closed in August 1945.

Llwynypia looking north towards Llwynypia Hospital

It was Llwynpia that as a child I would go and stay with my Aunty Mary and Uncle Davey Pattimore who lived in Harcombe Road. I have fond memories of these days when the sheep would roam the paths and roads and quite often you would wake up with sheep in your garden.

My Cousin Alan and I along with my Brother Raymond would spend hours playing on the mountain and waxing cardboard to slide down the mountain.

Each day we would do some chores to earn 3d so that we could go to the local sweet shop called Nellie's in William Street the next road down from us. This shop was in the front room of the house as was many shops in the Rhondda in those days. How I loved those days and even now when going to the Rhondda I say I'm going home

Words from Meditations

While I was meditating this morning these words came to me

Hello can you give me some time
I'd like to tell of my time in the mines
From dawn to dusk
Amongst black coal dust
Never knowing what will happen next
As the sweat runs down your neck
The dust enters my lungs
This is where my story began
We'd work hard day and night
Still we had to fight for what's right
Times ahead will be hard
I still have faith in my union card
If we strike there'll be no pay
How will we cope with bills to pay?
The 9th of January was strike day

It was to last for fifty days
It ended with us getting better pay
But at what price did we pay
They closed the mines it was a shock but a relief
Still it left a Valley in grief

Penrhys

Penrhys is a village in the county borough of Rhondda Cynon Taf village in the Wales, situated high on a hillside overlooking both valleys of Rhondda Fawr and Rhondda Fach. It is situated around 1,100 ft. above sea level and is a district of Tylorstown. Up to the late 16th century, Penrhys was one of the holiest sites for Christian pilgrims in Wales.

The site of Penrhys has a rich religious history dating back to mediaeval times, there little evidence of settlements other than farmsteads can be traced to the area. Penrhys is significant for a mediaeval monastery, the holy shrine of "Our Lady" built at the holy spring of Ffynnon Fair. During the early 16th century an antiquarian wrote during his visit to the area that he saw *"Penrise Village, where the Pilgrimage was"*, suggesting that a settlement had built up in the area. History reports that in 1538 the shrine was destroyed during the English reformation, and the area appeared to fall into decline. Until the arrival of industrialisation in the Rhondda Valley during the 19th century interest in the religious history of Penrhys increased. An archaeological dig at the old chapel was carried out in 1912 and a new statue of the Virgin Mary was unveiled in 1953. In February 1927 the first burial took place at Penrhys cemetery.

In 1904 the mining population of Rhondda was over 110,000 and still expanding rapidly. Although a 'fever hospital' had been constructed in nearby Ystrad the threat of smallpox had become a concern to the Medical Officer of Health, who recommended a separate containment site. In 1906 the Health Committee purchased three acres of land at

36

Penrhys, chosen for its accessibility to both Rhondda valleys and its distance from other habitable buildings. The smallpox hospital was completed in 1907 and at first served the Rhondda and later all of South Wales. In the 1970s the building was deemed unnecessary and was burnt to the ground by the South Wales Fire Service in 1971.

In 1927 Penrhys was chosen as the starting point for 'Red Sunday in Rhondda Valley' hunger march. The march was organized by the south Wales Miners federation and the Rhondda District, this lost support due to opposition from the TUC. It was supported by the Communist party and the march went ahead supported by 270 marchers.

The village of Penrhys that exists today was first developed in 1966 as a new modern council housing development. Built between 1966 and 1969, Peter the houses consisted of short two and three story terraces with cement rendered concrete walls and Mon pitch roofs. When it was officially opened in 1968, it consisted of 951 houses, at the time the largest public-sector housing venture in Wales.

One of the innovative features of Penrhys village was the district heating system; under an agreement with the National coal board, water was heated in a central coal-fired boiler, and a network of insulated pipes served each house with space heating and hot water for domestic use, with the cost of heating included in the rent. This was designed and built during a period of low bulk energy costs, but proved very expensive following the Oil Crisis of 1973 which increased the cost of energy. As heating cost increases had to be absorbed into the rent, the village became uneconomic for those residents who were not reliant on state benefits (which paid housing costs), and many of those in employment left the estate to move to other housing where they could have more control of heating costs.

The outflow of employed residents led to a process of social engineering whereby those on unemployment or other state benefits were relocated into Penrhys from other council run estates (with the initial prospect of them a saving on separate heating costs). As a result of the concentration of socially impoverished residents during the 1970s and 1980s the village gained a poor reputation and was seen by many as an undesirable location. In an attempt to rejuvenate the village, the Priority Estate Program was undertaken in the late 1980s with all houses refurbished and environmental improvements made throughout the community. This, though, proved unsuccessful as the reputation of Penrhys was so low that new occupants could not be found; this led to newly refurbished houses being vandalized as they stood empty. This in turn fueled the area's negative reputation.

By the 1990s the local authorities had begun a relocation program for Penrhys, with many buildings demolished once the tenants had been relocated. By the early 21st century much of the village had been demolished, leaving around 300 buildings remaining.

Our Lady of Penrhys

The mountain race

As a child the mountain I would climb
On a piece of card I would race down
Rushing through the ferns
To be first I'd yearn
Keeping us happy hours a day
The mountain was a safe place to play
Then just before dark
We'd go to the park
But when the streetlight shone
It was time to go home
Time for bed with a sadden face
Tomorrow I'll have another race

Gelli

Early and industrial history

The village of Gelli is known to get its name from a farm that was once found in the area, which translates from the welsh Language roughly as 'small wood or copse'. Before the industrialisation of the area the area consisted of few settlements in the area, mainly small agricultural and farm buildings. On Archeological digs in the area these have provided proof of earlier populations, mainly Bronze Age, though Gelli does house one of only two definite Romano-British finds in the Rhondda Valleys. Roman finds in the uplands of Glamorgan are scarce, but the settlement at Hen Dre'r Gelli, excavated in 1903, is the only undefended settlement of its type in the Rhondda. A lengthy archaeological report was published in 1906, but little remains of the site, with much destroyed during the construction of the Nant y Gwyddon refuse tip.

The farmlands of 19th century Gelli were owned by absentee landlords, who would gain from selling the areas when coal exploration began. The first pit sunk in Gelli was in the 1870s, undertaken by the firm owned by Edmund Thomas and George Griffiths. The Gelli Colliery was then purchased by brothers, John and Richard Cory who deepened the pit further. The colliery suffered a mining accidents when a gas explosion in 1893 took the lives of five miners. Subsequently the pit was sold to the Powell Duffryn Company, who owned the mine until the nationalization of the mining industry in 1947. A second pit was opened by David Davies in 1877, the Eastern Colliery, though this closed in 1937.

Moden Gelli

Like all villages in the Rhondda Valley, since the end of the coal mining industry, the area has suffered an economic depression with a history of unemployment higher than the national average. With little employment in the area apart from retail services many people commute to work outside the valley.

Gelli, which is adjoined by the communities of Ton Pentre and Ystrad, experiences fairly heavy levels of road traffic, with the B4223 – linking Llwynpia to Cwmparc– passing through the village. Gelli has also suffered in the past from flooding, owing to its low-lying level in relation to the River Rhondda, and after two serious floods in 1960 and 1970, the council responded by making improvements to the flood defenses known as the Rhondda Wall.

Gelli (Nantgwyddon) was also home to a landfill site which has been at the center of controversial reports connecting it with birth defects in children born in the nearby vicinity. The reports resulted in a full scale environmental report, and the decision by the local authorities to cease the dumping of domestic waste at the site.

The river Rhondda showing flood defenses at Gelli

Sirens Sound

Its ten past eight the sirens sound
There must be miners trapped under ground
Please God let them be found
There is silence to listen for sound
Tapping has been heard
The news comes through
As rescuers join the queue
Cage by cage the team go down
To the broken shaft below the ground
The rafters are weak and begin to creek
As water begins to leak

Twenty men are found at last
Let's get them out of this pit shaft
As they arrive at the top
It's clear to see the horrors of a miner's lot
Men are broken but spirits are high
For today in this mine no one died

Ystrad

Ystrad (also known as Ystrad Rhondda or Ystrad-Rhondda) is a community and village which lays in the Rhondda Fawr valley, Rhondda Cynon taf, Wales As a community and ward Ystrad contains the neighboring district of Gelli. Ystrad is a former coal mining village which was once housed the most profitable collieries belonging to the Cory brothers.

Ystrad is long and narrow, a main road where most amenities can be found, and a series of smaller residential streets lined with the terraces associated with the area. The majority of housing stock is the classic South Wales Valleys terrace with infills of new build

The Rhondda Fawr River runs through the village, separating it from Gelli on the southern bank.

Like most former coal mining communities in the South Wales Coalfield Ystrad is remarkably self-contained. There is a very strong community in Ystrad Rhondda - a common feature of these mining towns. The Ystrad Rhondda Railway station is on the Rhondda line.

The oldest Baptist chapel in the Rhondda, and originally known as Ynysfach Chapel, Nebo was located at Ystrad. It was demolished in the early 1980s.

Ystrad is home to rugby union team Ystrad Rhondda RFC, a Welsh Rugby Union affiliated team who play in the 2nd tier of the Welsh rugby leagues.

Ystrad Rhondda and Bodringalic Schools.

View of Ystrad

Where I belong
The Rhondda Valley is where my heart belongs
I haven't visited for far too long
Next Friday I am going home
To the land of my Fathers
I'll catch up with family and make new friends
Some who live at the Valleys End?
To be there for such a short time
I hope I see everyone in time
I class the Rhondda as my home
A place where I never feel alone

Ton Pentre

Ton Pentre is a village in the Rhondda Valley set in the county borough of Rhondda Cynon Taf Wales. Ton Pentre, is a former industrial coal mining village, is a district of the community of Pentre. The old district of Ystradyfodwg was named after the church at Ton Pentre. Ton Pentre is, is perhaps, best known for an incident in 1924, when The Duke of York (later to become King George V1 of the United Kingdom and the British dominions) played a round of golf with the General Secretary of the miners federation of Great Britain

Early and industrial history

One of the earliest recorded settlements in Ton Pentre is an Iron Age hillfort and can be found at Maindy Camp. Although initially believed to have been from the Bronze Age period, the camp was misidentified due to items from a Bronze Age cairn that were found inside the camp perimeter.

The area on which Ton Pentre now stands was originally the site of a cluster of platform houses or hafodi; small farming buildings, occupied only during the summer months. The site was later settled by a farm and a few cottages, known as 'Y Ton' ('meadow') the site was owned by absentee landlord. To distinguish the area from nearby Tonypandy, it became known as Ton Pentre.

When it became viable to mine anthracite coal in deep shaft pits in the mid-19th century, many pits were sunk in the Rhondda valley, one of which was located in Ton Pentre - The Maindy Colliery. It was the individual collieries that were at the heart of the separate 'villages' that emerged on the valley floor as they were the major employers in the area. At the height of the coal mining industry Ton Pentre was home to a few thousand people living in high density terraced houses that spanned the whole valley.

David Davies and his last half crown

The largest colliery in the area, Maindy Colliery, was established in Ton-Pentre when the first mine was sunk by David Davies & Partners in 1864.

Davies had rented land in the Rhondda Fawr and had searched for a workable seam for 15 months. When he had finally run out of money he gathered his workforce together and paid them their final wages. Digging his hand into his pocket he took out a single half Crown saying, "There you are. That's all I've got". Someone in the crowd replied, "'We'll have that as well" and Davies impulsively threw his last coin into the crowd. The gathering of men was so impressed by this gesture, the men agreed to continue working for another seven days without pay showing they believed that coal could be found. On the seventh day of digging with no pay, a massive seam of the best-quality steam coal was finally found.

The mine was near closure in 1866 when the Six Feet seam was discovered. This sustained production of coal until 1948, when mining ceased at the colliery, though it remained open as a ventilation shaft for other mines.

The colliery in 1910.

Ton Pentre Maindy Colliery

Pentre

The area which is now Pentre was made up of several scattered farms tended by tenant farmers for absentee landlords. Like most of the early farms in the Valley they were run by absentee landlords who would make a profit at the beginning of the industrial start of the Rhondda. With the discovery, in the early 19th century, of economically viable coal deposits in Dinas Rhondda it was not long until expeditions reached the mid valleys. In 1857 Edward Curteis of Liandaff leased the mineral rights of Tyr-y-Pentre from Griffith Llewellyn of Baglan and soon had two levels opened, the Pentre and Church. During the early part of 1864 deeper shafts had been sunk by the Pentre Coal Company. The mines in the Pentre were some of the most profitable of all the collieries in the Rhondda.

By the early 20th century, Pentre was a busy town and the main shopping area for the upper Rhondda and was also the center for local government, with the local council offices built in Llewellyn Street in 1882. Pentre is also home to St Peters Church (1890), the 'Cathedral of the Rhondda', the largest religious building in either valley.

Two of the most notable businesses to have existed in the Rhondda were both formed in Pentre; the Pentre Breweries and the Rhondda Engine Works.

St Peter's Church 2008

From the Valleys

As a child from the Valley's I came
I remember the games I played
The streets were safe to be out late
I moved far away I sometimes wish I had stayed
Everyone in the Valley knew each other
Through the mines and its community
I've been thinking of the Valley of late
I remember collecting bits of coal from the slag heaps
On the mountain side they were so steep
The Rhondda Valley is in my soul
This is what makes my life whole

Cwmparc is a Village and a district of the community of Treorchy, in the Rhondda Valley Wales.

History

There is evidence of (and logic for) a medieval park, or hunting preserve, in the enclosed area called Parc Cwm Brychiniog. It lies in the cwmwd (in English 'commote') of Glyn Rhondda, a Welsh lordship centered on a motte and bailey castle at the confluence of the Rhondda Fawr and Nant y Clydach (below the town of Tonypandy) and now known as Ynys y Crug. Little of this structure remains, the motte having been largely destroyed by the building of Taff Vale railway in the 19th Century and the Tonypandy by-pass in the 20th Century. The land below cwm was subsequently divided into four farms in Tudor times, one of which was called Parc Uchaf and another Parc Isaf. Thus the area became known as Cwmparc and its stream Nant Cwmparc (Cwm being the Welsh for valley). With the development of the coal mining village in this part of the south Wales Valley in the 19th century, the village also became known as Cwmparc. Above the present village is the mountain pass - Bwlch y Clawdd - leading to the Ogwr and Afan valleys.

With a population of about five thousand. The Parc [colliery] and, further down the valley, the Dare colliery, and the constant processions of [coal]-laden trucks running down the railway that flanked the Parc River.

Parc and Dare workingmen's hall

WWII bombing

On the night of 29 April 1941, during World War 2, Cwmparc was bombed by the German Lufwaffe. There were many casualties with 27 dead, three of whom were evacuees; all members of the same family. The evacuees were all buried in the same grave in Treorchy Cemetery. This event was the biggest loss of life that the Rhondda suffered in a single night of WWII bombing. It was known that the Lufwaffe would drop land mines on the mountains by parachute my Father once told me of a Bevan Boy who saw such a parachute coming down. Thinking it was a German the Bevan Boy jumped on this mine and was killed

My Saddest Day

As a 10 Year old it was my saddest day
When a mountain slipped and took a school away
To all the children and teachers that went to Heaven that day
My thoughts remain with you even thou I'm far away
I remember in assembly the news was broke to us
As a hush fell over all of us
My teacher knew I was from Wales
As my tears began to swell
To one side I was taken
Clearly I was shaken
Now that I am 58 I still cannot escape
The saddest day of my life
When so many was taken away

Treorchy

Treorchy is a village, although it used to be and still has characteristics of a town, in the county borough of Rhondda Cynon Taf Wales, lying in the Rhondda Fawr valley. Treorchy is also one of the 16 communities of the Rhondda, taking in the near villages of Cwmparc and Ynyswen.

History

Like many Villages and Towns in the Rhondda it takes its name from areas or history of the area. Places like farms and land areas

Treorchy is said to take its name from the stream that flows from the mountainside above the village into the River Rhondda; the 1875 Ordnance Survey map of the area refers to the stream is referred to as 'Nant Orky'. The word Gorchi possibly comes from the Welsh word Gorchwy, suggesting a stream marking a boundary. Prior to industrialisation the tithe maps of the area show an unpopulated area of scattered farmhouses, such as Abergorchwy, Tile-du, and Glyn Coli. The area was predominantly meadows, pastures and woodland and farmed by tenant farmers such as Walter Edwards, Llewellyn Lewis and Mary Evans. Much of the land, in common with most of the Rhondda at that time, was owned by one of the great families of Glamorgan The discovery of coal in the Rhondda Valley transformed the locality and within the decades after 1851 Treorchy became a densely populated industrial town.

Treorchy was established when the Abergorki Colliery, situated in Cwm Orci to the north, was opened as a level in 1859 by a Mr Huxham, a former manager of the Bute Merthyr Colliery. The mine was later sold to J.H. Insole of Cymmer in 1862.The first deep mines in Treorchy was sunk in the 1860s by David Davies of Llandinam who would later own the cean coal company. The initial development of the town was linear, based on the main road through the valley, but by 1875 a grid pattern of streets was emerging.

The town grew around the Coal mining industry during the late nineteenth and early twentieth century, but by the end of the twentieth century all the local pits had closed creating an economic downturn in the community.

Language

Before they became industrialized the Rhondda was a Welsh-speaking community and the Welsh language continued to be widely spoken in the valley, and particularly in the upper villages of the Rhondda until the mid-twentieth century. Many of the original migrants to the Rhondda were from rural Wales but a higher proportion came from England than was the case in those valleys that were industrialized earlier. In 1901 64.4% of the population of the Rhondda Urban District were recorded as Welsh-speaking but this proportion fell to 56.6% by 1911.

The proportion of Treorchy's population able to speak Welsh fell to around 45% in 1921 and to less than 30% by 1851. In 1971, 20.3% of Treorchy's population were recorded as Welsh-speaking, which was higher proportion than in any other ward within the Rhondda Municipal Borough.

Employment

Treorchy was, for many years, a town that relied on the coal mines such as Abergorki, Tylecoch, Parc and Dare collieries. All of the collieries had closed by the end of the 1970s, leaving many to find new work. Treorchy became a commuter village, with the working population seeking employment in the larger towns and cities that surround it, such as Cardiff and Bridgend. The work in Treorchy now is mostly retail.

Parc and Dare Hall 2008

My Beautiful Rhondda

My beautiful Rhondda
Has always been in my heart
In my life it's played a big part
I remember the sheep that roamed the streets
The mountains that stand so tall
As a child I would climb them all
Looking down on the valley at night
The orange lights that twinkled so bright
The bus stop in Pentre where we'd meet at night
In those days as kids we did not fight
Up the mountain ran the hospital wall
We'd stand on it feeling tall
My beautiful Rhondda is in my heart
In my life it will always play a part

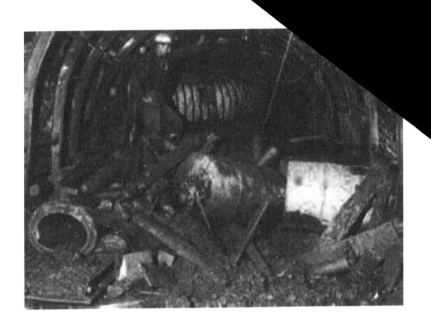

Broken Mine

As I'm trapped in this broken mine
I can't get you out of my mind
Will I see you again?
Will I be rid of this pain?
Just to see you one more time
Please God let me get out of this mine
A flicker of light from my lamp
I lay here cold and damp
I see your tears and sorrow
Faith I have I'll be out tomorrow
Am I the only one?
Where have all my Butty gone

ust stay awake
I'm to make
ote in coal
this hell hole

Treherbert

Treherbert is village and community situated at the head of the Rhondda Fawr valley in the county borough of Rhondda Cynon Taf Wales. Treherbert is a former industrial coal mining village which was at its economic peak between 1850 and 1920. Treherbert is the upper most community of the Rhondda Fawr and encompasses the districts of Blaencwn, Bleanrhondda Tynewydd and Pen-yr-englyn.

History

There is evidence of settlements in the Rhondda dating back to Celtic times, but prior to the industrial Revolution and the advent of coal mining the villages of Treherbert, Tynewydd, Blaenrhondda and Blaencwm consisted of a number of isolated rural farms and scattered homesteads. In 1841 there were only 218 people residing in the 'Middle hamlet of Treherbert', which had risen to 1,203 by 1861.

In August 1845, Cemsaerbren farm was brought for £11,000 to sink the first steam coal pit in the Rhondda valley. A trial pit was sunk from 1850, but progress was slow due to the fact that all equipment had to be carried over rough tracks by horse and cart from the Taf Vale Railway's then terminus at Dina. In April 1853 the first seam of what was called the Bute Merthyr Colliery was struck at a depth of 125 yards, and production was begun in early 1855.

Parish records showed the first use of the name Treherbert from January 1855, commemorating the Herbert earls of Pembroke, one of the ancestors of Bute family the first 38 wagons of steam coal were transported from the newly extended Taff Vale Railway station at Gellialed (Ystrad) Cardiff Docks on 21 December 1855. Installation of the railway line facilitated the rapid expansion of the village, and the need to build new houses, the first rows of which were built at Bute Street, Dumfries Street, and Baglan Street.

Present day

During the early 21st century many of the buildings of 'old' Treherbert were demolished; including Treherbert Hospital, Treherbert Police Station, Dunraven School (Tynewydd), Blaencwm School, Blaenrhondda School, Penyrenglyn Infants and Junior School,

Businesses in Treherbert have also joined together to create the Treherbert Chamber of Trade, Commerce and Tourism. The group aims to help promote local business life whilst improving the community as a whole and increasing tourism to the Upper Rhondda with notable sites like PenPych Mountain.

PenPych Mountain was mentioned earlier in this book in the form of a poem

Transport

The main road in the northerly direction out of Treherbert is the a4061 Rhigos Mountain Road.

Treherbert Library

Bleancwm

Bleancwm is a district in Treherbert Rhondda Fawr at the head of the Rhondda Valley

Before the industrialisation of the Rhondda, Blaencwm was a forested. Research of the area has shown evidence of Mesolithic and Neolithic human activity, mostly through the discovery of basic hunting, foraging and tool making items. Blaencwm is also the site of three ruinous 16th century hafotai (summer houses; these being small agricultural dwellings discovered on the north-east slope of the village. Of all the hafotai discovered in the Rhondda the most important is *Lluest* discovered in Blaencwm and proof of the agricultural history of the area.

It was in the 19th century with the coming of the Taff Vale Railway coal mine began opening in the upper Rhondda Fawr. Two mines were sunk in Blaencwm, the first was the Dunraven Colliery opened by Thomas Joseph's Dunraven United Collieries in 1865. This business went in liquidation in 1866 eventually taken over by Watts and Company in 1872. Who remained the owners until 1913 when it was purchased again, this time by the Cory Brothers, it changed its name to Tydraw Colliery. It closed in 1956. The second colliery, Glenrhondda (known locally as the Hook and Eye due to its reputation for improvisation), was opened in 1911 by Glenavon Garw Collieries. The mine was served by the Rhondda and Swansea Bay Railway which would travel through the Rhondda Tunnel. This pit was closed by the National Coal Board in 1966.

Blaenrhondda is a village in the county borough of Rhondda Cynon Taf Wales, lying at the head the Rhondda Fawr valley. Blaenrhondda is a very small village and is part of the community of Treherbert.

History

The earliest evidence of people habitating the area are the remains of an iron age settlement of several roundhouses grouped together in an obvious community, known as Hen Dre'r Mynydd. The dry wall layout of the ruinous site has led archeologists to believe that the people who lived in the area were early farmers] It has been identified as the largest undefended Iron Age settlement in south east Wales.

Before the industrialisation of the Rhondda Valleys in the late 19th century, Blaenrhondda was an agricultural area and sparsely populated. With the coming of the Coal industry two mines were sunk in the locality. The first was the North Dunraven, also known as the Blaenrhondda, sunk in 1859, followed by Fernhill Colliery around 1871. The Dunraven closed in the 1920s but the Fernhill was still operating as late as 1978. In an attempt to break the monopoly of the Taff Vale Railway and the Cardiff docks, a tunnel was constructed through Mynydd Blaengwynfy to link up with the Rhondda and Swansea Bay Railway to supply coal to the Swansea Docks for export. The resulting tunnel, at a length of 3,300 yards was the longest rail tunnel in Wales and the seventh longest in Britain. Due to an issue with the weight the engines could pull, the rail link was never the success it was hoped to be, though it did prove popular with day-trippers from the Rhondda, visiting Swansea and the Gower. The station was closed in 1970.

In the hills above Blaenrhondda lies Bleanrhondda Road Cutting, a Site of special scientific interest. It was given this status for its rock exposures showing sediments that formed on the flood plain of a river delta during the Carboniferous period, approximately 310 million years ago.

Glyngwyn Road and Pen Pych

My Dad

Here's comes my dad carrying coal
Looking another day old
Skin so dark from the dust
Cloths covered with tints of rust
Hot tin bath ready and waiting
Straight in with no hesitating
In front of the fire with its warm glow
I wish to the mines I didn't have to go
In the mines there is no glory
Just tales of sad stories
But a miner I have to be
If my family I want to feed
So tomorrow I'll do it again
I wish my mining days would end.

Inspired by my Cousin Carol

71

72

Rhondda Fach

Ynyshir

Ynyshir is a village and a community located in the Rhondda Valley, within Rhondda Cynon Taf, South Wales. The way in which the villages got their name mostly comes from farms in the area, falling within the historic parishes of Ystradyfodwg and Llanwynno. The community of Ynyshir lies between the small adjoining village of Wattstown and the larger town of neighboring Porth. In the village of Ynyshir boasts its own library, post office, and doctors surgery and a number of shops and other significant amenities, although these represent a fraction of the businesses which once fronted the main road Ynyshir Road during the village's heyday. It is also home to local football teams Ynyshir Albions and Ynyshir and Wattstown Boys Club.

History

Ynyshir used to be an agricultural area till the mid-18th century it was not till 1840s that the first deep coal mine was sunk in the village, representing the first colliery to be opened in the Rhondda Fach valley, and consequently Ynyshir also represents the earliest colliery settlement of the valley.

It was along the west bank of the river Fach that the initial development of the village began within the parish of Ystradyfodwg on the land that Ynyshir took its name Ynyshir farm, later followed by the development east of the river within the parish of Llanwonno on land owned by

Maendy and Penrhiw farms. By 1900 much of the village which is evident today was in place.

In 1841 the Taff Vale Railway reached neighboring Dinas and with the train came far greater commercial opportunities for prospective colliery owners, with the first section of the Rhondda Fach Branch of the Taff Vale railway being marked by the extension of the railway from Porth and Dinas to Ynyshir in 1849.

Ynyshir was home to several chapels/churches, namely - Ainon Chapel (Welsh Baptist), Bethany Chapel (English Baptist), Moriah Chapel (Calvinistic Methodist), St Anne's (Church in Wales), Saron Chapel (Welsh Independent), Ynyshir Welsh Wesleyan Methodist Chapel, Bethel Chapel (Welsh Baptist), Penuel Chapel (English Independent), Tabernacle Chapel (Congregational Methodist) and Ynyshir English Wesleyan Methodist Chapel.

Ynyshir Welfare Band played at the Millennium Centre, Cardiff

In 2009 the new modern community Primary school opened at a cost of £5.5 million located on Llanwonno road this was to replace the previous Ynyshir Junior School and later in 2010 also replaced the old Ynyshir Infants School off Gynor Place.

Industrialisation

The first deep mine to be sank was by owners Shepherd and Evans in 1845. The mine was sold to Francis Crawshay to supply the Crawshay Ironworks in Treforest. The Ynyshir colliery would be followed by the Ynyshir Steam Collicry, Standard 1 pit in 1875 and Standard 2 pit in 1876 and then in 1904 the Lady Lewis opened, which was later connected underground to the Lewis Merthyr Consolidated Collieries which today is the Rhondda Heritage Park at Hafod (Trehaford).

In 1896, two local brothers invented carbonated soft-drink Lurvills Delight, they used the profits to rise money to help 150 local mining families to immigrate to the United States. Production ceased in 1910, due a local shortage of dock leaves.

An Angel

An Angel came to me today
It showed a light to show the way
For in the dark I seemed to be
My Butty I could not see
Was that them blasting coal
To get to this tiny hole
How long have I been here?
A voice said rest now my dear The Angels are near
I saw my children happily playing
While my wife was praying

I guess this is how it ends
The lights growing bright I have no fight
With the Angels I'll sleep tonight
I won't be going home
But I did not die alone
There is no air I cannot breathe
The Angel said we must leave
Holding me by the hand
The Angel took me to a wonderful land
Time ran out for me today
Now with the Angels I play

Watts Town

Wattstown is a village located in the Rhondda Valley in the county borough of Rhondda Cynon Taf, Wales. Located in the Rhondda Fach valley it is a district of the community of Ynshir. Before the industrialization of wattstown the area was once little more than a wooded area, sparsely populated by farmsteads. With the coming of the coal industry Wattstown became a busy, densely populated village, but with the closure of the collieries Wattstown suffered an economic downturn that still affects the village today.

Wattstown is named after Edmund Hannay Watts, who at one time owned the National Colliery in Wattstown.

Early history and industrialisation

There is early evidence of human activity around what would become Wattstown is found on the hillside at Carn Y Wiwer, overlooking the village; a small grouping of Bronze age cairns are present and in the same vicinity are the remains of five platform houses; believed to be medieval farm house used seasonally. During the Napoleonic Wars the land around Carn Y Wiwer was cultivated by farmers to produce additional crops. Prior to industrialisation, the area that would become Wattstown was known as Pont Rhyd Y Cwch or Pont-Y-Cwtch.

Compared to other areas in the Rhondda, Wattstown was slow to be developed as a mining area. With the first deep mine not being sunk till the late 1870s the National Colliery, originally known as Cwtch Colliery before being renamed the Standard, and first appeared on the Inspectors'

Lists of Mines in 1880. The land on which the colliery was built, belonged to Crawshay Bailey and William Bailey, but the mine was owned by several different concerns, including the National Steam Coal Company and Watts & Company, who would give the village its name. Although Wattstown expanded to fulfill the working requirements of its colliery, it never expanded at the same rate as other areas. The village had its own church, dedicated to St. Thomas, built in 1896, schools, chapels and public houses, but its number of private residents was much lower than other similar settlements in the South Wales Valley.

National Colliery 1887 disaster

Wattstown was to suffer two mining disasters at the National Colliery. The first was on 18 February 1887, when the village was still known as 'Cwtch'. The accident occurred in-between the day and night shifts, which probably saved many lives as 200 men were yet to make their descent into the mine. The explosion was so powerful it damaged the Winding Gear which delayed the rescue by several hours. Once the rescuers were able to descend they managed to bring to the surface 38 men, 29 of whom were uninjured. In total, the death toll counted thirty men and boys, with a total of 12 injured. Although an inquest jury could not come to a conclusion to the cause of the explosion, in his report to the Secretary of State for the Home Department, F.A. Basanquet, placed the cause of the disaster as an explosive cap being fired in an area where there had been a buildup of flammable gas.

National Colliery 1905 disaster

It was On the 11 July 1905, just four months after

the Cambrian Colliery disaster at Clydach Vale, an explosion at the National Colliery in Wattstown resulted in the deaths of 120 men and boys. Only three people were rescued from the mine, but two would later die of their injuries, leaving Matthew Davies as the lone survivor. The report into the cause of the disaster was undertaken by the Inspector of Mines, which concluded that the explosion was caused by illegal use of blasting material underground. Shortly before the explosion occurred, the master sinker had requested blasting cable and a battery to charge the shot. The manager, Mr. Meredith had entered the mine a quarter of an hour before the explosion and was amongst the list of fatalities.

Amongst the messages of condolences received at Wattstown was a message from King Edward Vll. On the day of the funeral, the streets were lined by thousands of mourners and the funeral cortège was reported as being over four miles (6 km) long.

Aerial view of Watts Town

Going Home

Home to wales I went for the weekend
Meeting family and new friends
Aunty Mary lovely as ever
The mountains covered in heather
Sarah and Neil thank you for your gift
I enjoyed going down in the pit lift
Carol and Robert you have a lovely place
I could sit on that beach with a happy face
Alan Annette Hayley I also saw
As the clouds over the Rhondda they soared
Di and Paul it was nice to meet you
I will never forget that sea view
Lisa and Paul thank you for the tea
It meant a lot to Charlie and me
Greg I remember you small
Now you are standing tall
To my family I never got to meet
Next time your first I will greet
On cardboard we thought of sliding the mountain
Taking us back to our childhood excitement
Sadly it will have to wait to next time
As I was rapidly running out of time
Drinks in the pub and caravan
As I thought of Calon LAN
Emma it was a short stop
It a shame your mam was at the chip shop
Down Lewis Merthyr pit meant a lot to me
As visions of past family I could see
A good time was had by all
Even if those mountains seem tall

Tylorstown

Tylorstown (Welsh Pendyrus) is a Village and Community located in the Rhondda valley, in the county borough of Rhondda Cynon Taf Wales. It was founded by Alfred Tylor who set up an early coal mining operation in the location in the mid-19th century.

The last working mine in the village closed in the 1960s setting off a long period of economic decline which worsened following the 1984–85 National miners' strike which resulted in pits in nearby locations such as Meardy closing. The local passenger train line closed in the 1960s following the Beeching Axe which also limited the prospects of easy commuting Cardiff.

It is neighbored by the villages of Bleanllechau, Ferndale Penrhys, Pontygwaith, and Stanleytown.

Social and economic standing

Tylorstown is a typical small ex-mining village in the Rhondda Fach valley.

The Porth relief road terminates at neighboring Tylorstown due to the topography of the Rhondda Fach, which is a narrow valley with steep sides and limited flat land on the valley floor. The construction of the Porth relief road started off with an estimate of £33m but by 2009, the project had cost £97.6m being a major civil-engineering project many years in the planning and two and a half years in the execution.

Tylorstown

In My Heart

The Rhondda is truly in my heart
On Sundays really didn't want to part
So much fun in such a short time
I even got to go down a mine
We'll keep a welcome in the hillside
Is truly a welsh thing
A welcome second to none
Was given by everyone
Memories I will cherish for life
As I drove home to my loving wife
Thank you family and the Rhondda
My heart will yearn for you even longer

Ferndale (*Glynrhedynog*) is a small town located in the Rhondda Valley in the county borough of Rhondda Cynon Taf, Wales. Neighboring Villages are Blaenllechau, Meardy and Tylorstown. Ferndale was industrialized in the mid-19th century when the first coal mine shaft was sunk in 1857 and was the first community to be intensively industrialized in the Rhondda Valley.

History

In Welsh Ferndale is known as Glynrhedynog, the name of one of the old farms on which the town is built. In its infancy Glynrhedynog was also known as Trerhondda after the name of the first large chapel to be built in the town. The naming of settlements after chapels was widespread in Wales at the time, as is shown in village names such as Bethesda, Beulah and Horeb, but neither Glynrhedynog nor Trerhondda was destined to be used for long.

The Welsh word Glynrhedynog is made from the words "glyn" meaning valley and "rhedynog" meaning ferny, and so coal from the Glynrhedynog pits was marketed as Ferndale coal, a much easier name for English buyers to assimilate. The Ferndale pits are what drew the workforce and their families to the area, and by the 1880s "Ferndale" was well established as a thriving town. With the phasing in of bilingual road signs from the late 1980s onwards, the name Glynrhedynog gradually reappeared and is now the officially designated Welsh language name for Ferndale. The Welsh language is on the increase in Ferndale after the village adopted the English language during the industrial revolution. A Welsh language school is situated near the park and the school is named after the park's lake, 'Llyn-y-Forwyn.' (The Maiden's Lake)

Industry

The pioneer of coal mining at Ferndale was David Davis of Blaengwawr, Aberdare who already had an extensive colliery business in the neighboring Aberdare Valley. His wealth enabled him to engage in costly but unsuccessful singings in the Rhondda Fach in the 1860s until he finally struck a good seam at Ferndale.

Ferndale Colliery disasters

Two large coal mining colliery disasters occurred in Ferndale during the 19th century. The first occurred on 8 November 1867, when an underground explosion killed 178 miners at the Ferndale Colliery owned by David Davis and Sons Ltd. The second disaster happened on 10 June 1869 when a further explosion resulted in the death of 53 miners.

Modern Ferndale

Ferndale has developed over recent years. Some new features have been added such as a new astro-turf field, car park and an all-weather cricket training enclosure. The

Early Photo of Ferndale

Dinas

Dinas colliery is my place of work
We dig the mine for all it's worth
Miners come up one by one
Father and son their work done
Skin blackened from dust below
Where we would blast the coal
Down to the cottages we walk home
Chilled through to the bone
Hot tin bath already ran
As I eat a semi stale bun
Once the bills are paid
With the rest the table is laid
We had no comforts like today
Only slag heaps for children to play
Time for bed I'll say goodnight
Tomorrow I'll miss another daylight

Maerdy is a village and community in the county borough of Rhondda Cynon Taf, and within the historic county boundaries of glamorgan Wales, lying at the head of the Rhondda Fach Valley.

History

"Maerdy" is a Welsh word meaning "house of the mayor", and may indicate a medieval origin. The "mayor" was the official also known as the reeve, usually the most affluent farmer in the area. However the original ancient Welsh meaning of Maerdy is Slave house. The name is found in several locations throughout Wales and may well indicate the site of Dark Age slave markets. The use of the word 'Mardy' in colloquial English to describe a sullen and sulky individual would appear to stem from the old Welsh word for slave.

The area grew from a farming community to town around the coal mining industry and the development of Mardy Colliery in the late 19th century, but its last pit shut in 1990. Maerdy was not originally an area of industrial confrontation, with the Cambrian mines of Pentre showing far more socialist ideals. This view would change by the mid to late 20th century when Maerdy became synonymous with working class syndicalism and solidarity. In the mid-twentieth century Maerdy was associated with the Communist Party of Great Britain and radical miners' leaders such as Arthur Horner and was known as Little Moscow. By the time of the Miner Strike in the 1980s, Maerdy was the location of one of the last working mines in the south Wales valleys, and the pictures of the returning

miners once the strike was resolved was one of the defining
moments of late 20th century Welsh history.

Aberfan

The time was about 9.15 am the last day of term, the sun was shining after two days of continuous rain on Friday, October 21, 1966 the waste tip above Aberfan started to loosen the waste tip slid down the mountainside into the mining village of Aberfan, near Merthyr Tydfil in South Wales. It's first casualty a farm cottage in its path, killing all the occupants. At Pantglas Junior School, just below, the children had just returned to their classes after singing All Things Bright and Beautiful at their assembly. It was sunny on the mountain but foggy in the village, with visibility about 50 yards. The tipping gang up the mountain had seen the slide start, but could not raise the alarm because their telephone cable had been repeatedly stolen. (The Tribunal of Inquiry later established that the disaster happened so quickly that a telephone warning would not have saved lives.) Down in the village, nobody saw anything, but everybody heard the noise. An eight-year-old at the school, remembered four years later:

It was a tremendous rumbling sound and all the school went dead. You could hear a pin drop. Everyone just froze in their seats. I just managed to get up and I reached the end of my desk when the sound got louder and nearer, until I could see the black out of the window. I can't remember any more but I woke up to find that a horrible nightmare had just begun in front of my eyes.

The slide engulfed the school and about 20 houses in the village before coming to rest. Then there was total silence. It was reported by a survivor who was trapped the silence that followed you couldn't hear a bird or a child'. 144 people died in the Aberfan disaster: 116 of them were school children. About half of the children at Pantglas Junior School, and five of their teachers, were killed.

So horrifying was the disaster that everybody wanted to do something. Hundreds of people stopped what they were doing, threw a shovel in the car, and drove to Aberfan to try and help with the rescue. It was futile; the untrained rescuers merely got in the way of the trained rescue teams. Nobody was rescued alive after 11am on the day of the disaster, but it was nearly a week before all the bodies were recovered. On this day I remember where I was.

I was ten years out and in my school assemble at meadow vale school Bracknell Berkshire, I remember the head master standing on the stage sullen faced and asking if there was anyone who was welsh or had family in wales, I standing next to my Brother Raymond and I put my hand up Raymond said you're not welsh I told him our father is welsh and that makes me welsh (to this day I still class myself as welsh and the Rhondda my home) as the head master started to tell the assemble what had happened I started to cry I didn't know much about Aberfan but I did know that children just like us in this assemble had been hurt or taken to heaven. This disaster was to remain with me all my life and I have made trips to Aberfan to pay my respects.

The Aberfan disaster was a catastrophic collapse of a colliery spoil tip in the Welsh village of Aberfan, near Merthyr Tydfil, on 21 October 1966, killing 116 children and 28 adults. It was caused by a build-up of water in the accumulated rock and shale, which suddenly started to slide downhill in the form of slurry.

Over 40,000 cubic meters of debris covered the

village in minutes, and the classrooms at Pantglas Junior School were immediately inundated, with young children and teachers dying from impact or suffocation. Many noted the poignancy of the situation: if the disaster had struck a few minutes earlier, the children would not have been in their classrooms, and if it had struck a few hours later, the school would have broken up for half-term.

Great rescue efforts were made, but the large numbers who crowded into the village tended to hamper the work of the trained rescue teams, and delayed the arrival of mineworkers from the Merthyr Vale Colliery. Only a few lives could be saved in any case.

The official inquiry blamed the National Coal Board for extreme negligence, and its Chairman, Lord Robens, for making misleading statements. Parliament soon passed new legislation about public safety in relation to mines and quarries.

Background

For 50 years up to 1966, millions of cubic meters of excavated mining debris from the National Coal Board's Merthyr Vale Colliery was deposited on the side of Mynydd Merthyr, directly above the village of Aberfan. Huge piles, or 'tips', of loose rock and mining spoil had been built up over a layer of highly porous sandstone that contained numerous underground springs, and several tips had been built up directly over these springs. Although local authorities had raised specific concerns in 1963 about spoil being tipped on the mountain above the village primary school, these were largely ignored by the NCB's area management.

Collapse

Early on the morning of Friday, 21 October 1966, after several days of heavy rain, a subsidence of about 3–6 meters occurred on the upper flank of colliery waste tip No. 7. At 9:15 a.m. more than 150,000 cubic meters of water-saturated debris broke away and flowed downhill at high speed. It was sunny on the mountain but still foggy in the village, with visibility only about fifty meters. The tipping gang working on the mountain saw the landslide start but were unable to raise the alarm because their telephone cable had been repeatedly stolen – although the official inquiry into the disaster later established that the slip happened so fast that a telephone warning would not have saved any lives.

The front part of the mass became liquefied and moved down the slope at high speed as a series of viscous surges. 120,000 cubic meters of debris were deposited on the lower slopes of the mountain, but a mass of over 40,000 cubic meters of debris smashed into the village in a slurry 12 meters (39 ft.) deep.

The slide destroyed a farm and twenty terraced houses along Moy Road and slammed into the northern side of the Pantglas Junior School and part of the separate senior school, demolishing most of the structures and filling the classrooms with thick mud and rubble up to 10 meters (33 ft.) deep. Mud and water from the slide flooded many other houses in the vicinity, forcing many villagers to evacuate their homes.

The pupils of Pantglas Junior School had arrived only minutes earlier for the last day before the half-term holiday. They had just left the assembly hall, where they had

95

been singing "All Things Bright and Beautiful", when a great noise was heard outside. Had they left the assembly for their classrooms a few minutes later the loss of life would have been significantly reduced, as they would not have reached their classrooms when the landslide hit: the classrooms were on the side of the building nearest the landslide.

Nobody in the village was able to see it, but everyone could hear the roar of the approaching landslide. Some at the school thought it was a jet about to crash and one teacher ordered his class to hide under their desks. Gaynor Minett, then an eight-year-old at the school, later recalled:

It was a tremendous rumbling sound and all the school went dead. You could hear a pin drop. Everyone just froze in their seats. I just managed to get up and I reached the end of my desk when the sound got louder and nearer, until I could see the black out of the window. I can't remember any more but I woke up to find that a horrible nightmare had just begun in front of my eyes.

After the landslide there was total silence. George Williams, who was trapped in the wreckage, remembered:

"In that silence you couldn't hear a bird or a child."

Rescue efforts

After the main landslide stopped, frantic parents rushed to the scene and began digging through the rubble, some clawing at the debris with their bare hands, trying to uncover buried children. Police from Merthyr Tydfil arrived soon after and took charge of the search and rescue operations; as news spread, hundreds of people drove to Aberfan to try to help, but their efforts were largely in vain.

A large amount of water and mud was still flowing down the slope, and the growing crowd of untrained volunteers further hampered the work of the trained rescue teams who were arriving. Hundreds of miners from local collieries rushed to Aberfan, especially from the nearby Merthyr Vale Colliery, as well as miners from Deep Navigation colliery and Taff Merthyr Colliery in the neighboring Taff Bergoed Valley, and also from pits across the South Wales coalfield, many in open lorries with their shovels in their hands, but by the time those miners reached the site, there was little they could do. A few children were pulled out alive in the first hour, but no survivors were found after 11 a.m.

By the next day, 2,000 emergency services workers and volunteers were on the scene, some of whom had worked continuously for more than 24 hours. Rescue work had to be temporarily halted during the day when water began pouring down the slope again, and because of the vast quantity and consistency of the spoil, it was nearly a week before all the bodies were recovered.

Bethania Chapel, 250 meters from the disaster site, was used as the temporary mortuary and missing person's bureau from 21 October until 4 November 1966 and its vestry was used to house volunteers and stretcher-bearers. The smaller Aberfan Calvinistic Chapel was used as a second mortuary from 22–29 October and became the final resting-place for the victims before their funerals.

Two doctors were given the job of making death certificates and examining the bodies; the causes of death were typically found to be asphyxia as, fractured skull or multiple crush injuries. A team of 400 embalmers arrived in Aberfan on Sunday and under police supervision they cleaned and prepared over 100 bodies and placed them in coffins obtained from South Wales, the Midlands, Bristol, and Northern Ireland. The bodies were released to the families from the morning of Monday 24 October. Due to the cramped conditions in the chapel/mortuary, parents could only be admitted one at a time to identify the bodies of their children. One mother later recalled being shown the bodies of almost every dead girl recovered from the school before identifying her own daughter.

The final death toll was 144. In addition to five of their teachers, 116 of the dead were children between the ages of 7 and 10 – almost half of the children at the Pantglas Junior School. Most of the victims were interred at the Bryntaf Cemetery in Aberfan in a joint funeral held on 27 October 1966, attended by more than 2,000 people.

Actions of Lord Robens

The chairman of the National Coal Board (NCB) at the time of the disaster was Lord Robens of Woldingham. Robens had been a senior union official in the 1930s and then served as a Labour MP, briefly becoming Minister of Power in the final days of the Attlee Labour government. His actions immediately after the Aberfan disaster and in the years that followed have been the subject of considerable criticism.

When word of the Aberfan disaster reached him, Robens did not immediately go to the scene; he instead went ahead with his investiture as Chancellor of the University of Surrey, and did not arrive at the village until the evening of the following day (Saturday). NCB officers covered up for Robens when contacted by the Secretary of State for Wales's cladwyn Hughes, falsely claiming that Robens was personally directing relief work when he was not present.

When he reached Aberfan, Robens told a TV reporter that nothing could have been done to prevent the slide, attributing it to 'natural unknown springs' beneath the tip, a statement which the locals knew to be false – the NCB had in fact been tipping on top of springs that were clearly marked on maps of the neighborhood, and where villagers had played as children.

Robens's actions in the period after the disaster. further damaged his reputation – he refused to allow Coal Board funds to be used for the removal of the remaining tips above Aberfan, instead appropriating a substantial sum from the public disaster relief fund to pay for the work.

Aftermath

The traumatic effects of the disaster on the village of Aberfan were wide-ranging and profound, as the first-hand accounts gathered by Iain McLean and Martin Johnes indicate. During the rescue operation, the shock and grief of parents and townspeople were exacerbated by the insensitive behavior of the media – one unnamed rescue worker recalled hearing a press photographer tell a child to cry for her dead friends because it would make a good picture. The Queen and the Duke of Edinburgh visited Aberfan on 29 October to pay their respects to those who had died. The Queen received a posy from a three-year-old girl with the inscription: "From the remaining children of Aberfan". Onlookers said she was close to tears.

Anger at the National Coal Board erupted during the inquest into the death of 30 of the children. The *Merthyr Express* reported that there were shouts of "murderers" as children's names were read out. When one child's name was read out and the cause of death was given as asphyxia and multiple injuries, the father said "No, sir, buried alive by the National Coal Board". The coroner replied: "I know your grief is much that you may not be realizing what you are saying" but the father repeated:

I want it recorded – 'Buried alive by the National Coal Board.' That is what I want to see on the record. That is the feeling of those present. Those are the words we want to go on the certificate.

Aberfan's social worker later noted that many people in the village were on sedatives but did not take them when it was raining because they were afraid to go to sleep, and that surviving children did not close their bedroom doors for fear of being trapped. An Aberfan doctor reported that although an expected surge in heart attacks did not occur, the trauma of the disaster manifested itself in other ways – the birth rate went up, alcohol-related problems increased, as did health problems for those with pre-existing illnesses, and many parents suffered breakdowns over the next few years.

Many suffered from the effects of guilt, such as parents who had sent children to school who did not want to go. Tensions arose between families who had lost children and those who had not. One of the surviving school children recalled that they did not go out to play for a long time because families who had lost children could not bear to see them, and they themselves felt guilty about the fact that they had survived.

A study into the long-term psychological effects of the disaster was published in the British Journal of Psychiatry in 2003. It found that half the survivors of the Aberfan disaster suffered from Post-Traumatic Stress Disorder (PTSD) at some time in their lives, that they were over three times more likely to have developed lifetime PTSD than a comparison group of individuals who had experienced other life-threatening traumas, and that 34% of survivors who took part in the study reported that they still experienced bad dreams or difficulty sleeping due to intrusive thoughts about the disaster.

Davies Inquiry

On 26 October 1966, after resolutions by both Houses of Parliament, the Secretary of State for Wales appointed a tribunal to inquire into the causes of and circumstances relating to the Aberfan disaster, chaired by respected Welsh barrister and Privy Councilor Lord Justice Edmunds Davies. Before the tribunal began, the UK Attorney General imposed restrictions on speculation in the media about the causes of the disaster.

The Tribunal sat for 76 days – the longest inquiry of its type in British history up to that time – interviewing 136 witnesses, examining 300 exhibits and hearing 2,500,000 words of testimony, which ranged from the history of mining in the area to the region's geological conditions.

Lord Robens made a dramatic appearance during the final days of the Tribunal to give testimony, at which point he conceded that the National Coal Board had been at fault; had this admission been made at the outset, much of the tribunal's inquiry would have been unnecessary

The Tribunal retired to consider its verdict on 28 April 1967. Its report, published on 3 August, found that the blame for the disaster rested entirely with the National Coal Board, and that the basic cause was the NCB's "total absence of [a] tipping policy".

The report also noted that the NCB was:

...following in the footsteps of their predecessors. They were not guided either by Her Majesty's inspectorate of Mines and Quarries or by legislation" and also found that there was "no legislation dealing with the safety of tips in force in this or any country, except in part of West Germany and in South Africa."

...we reject out of hand Mr. Ackner's observation that what has been revealed here is "callous indifference" by senior National Coal Board officials to the fears of a tip-slide expressed to them. Callousness betokens villainy, and in truth there are no villains in this harrowing story. In one way, it might possibly be less alarming if there were, for villains are few and far between. But the Aberfan disaster is a terrifying tale of bungling ineptitude by many men charged with tasks for which they were totally unfitted, of failure to heed clear warnings, and of total lack of direction from above. Not villains, but decent men, led astray by foolishness or by ignorance or by both in combination, are responsible for what happened at Aberfan. That, in all conscience, is a burden heavy enough for them to have to bear without the additional brand of villainy.

Blame for the disaster rests upon the National Coal Board. This is shared, though in varying degrees, among the NCB headquarters, the South Western Divisional Board, and certain individuals ... The legal liability of the NCB to pay compensation of the personal injuries, fatal or otherwise, and damage to property, is incontestable and uncontested.

The specific cause of the collapse was found to have been a build-up of water in the pile; when a small rotational slip occurred, the disturbance caused the saturated, fine material of the tip to liquefy (thixotropy) and flow down the mountain.

In 1958, the tip had been sited on a known stream (as shown on earlier Ordnance Survey maps) and had previously suffered several minor slips. Its instability was known both to colliery management and to tip workers, but very little was done about it. Merthyr Tydfil Borough Council and the National Union of Mineworkers were cleared of any wrongdoing.

The Tribunal found that repeated warnings about the dangerous condition of the tip had been ignored, and that colliery engineers at all levels had concentrated only on conditions underground. In one passage, the Report noted:

We found that many witnesses … had been oblivious of what lay before their eyes. It did not enter their consciousness. They were like moles being asked about the habits of birds.

The Tribunal also found that the tips had never been surveyed, and right up to the time of the landslide they were continuously being added to in a chaotic and unplanned manner. The disregard of the NCB and the colliery staff for the unstable geological conditions and its failure to act after previous smaller slides were found to have been major factors that contributed to the catastrophe.

The NCB was ordered to pay compensation to the families at the rate of £500 per child. Nine senior NCB staff were named as having some degree of responsibility for the accident, but no NCB staff were ever demoted, sacked or prosecuted, and Lord Robens and the entire Board of the NCB retained their positions.

Following the publication of the Report, Lord Robens wrote to the then Minister of Power, Richard Marsh, offering his resignation. Although Robens had a combative relationship with the government and several cabinet ministers argued strongly that he should go, in September 1967 the Prime Minister Harold Wilson and Marsh rejected Robens's resignation offer. According to Ronald Dearing, then a senior member of staff at the Ministry of Power, who briefed Marsh on the matter, the fact that Robens was "taking the coal industry through a period of painful contraction without big strikes" and the strong support for him within the coal industry and the union movement were crucial to the decision to retain him.

Disaster fund

The public demonstrated their sympathy by donating money, with little idea of how it would be spent. Donations flooded in to the appeal and within a few months, nearly 90,000 contributions had been received, totaling £1,606,929 (2008:£21.4 million).

The management of this fund caused considerable controversy over the years. Many aspects of the aftermath of the Aberfan Disaster remained hidden until 1997, when the British Public Records Office released previously embargoed documents under the thirty year rule. These documents revealed new information about the machinations of Lord Robens, the NCB and the Charity Commission in the wake of the Aberfan Disaster.

At one point the charity Commission planned to insist that before any payment was made to bereaved parents, each case should be reviewed to ascertain if the parents had been close to their children and were thus likely to be suffering mentally. At another meeting, the Commission threatened to remove the Trustees of the Disaster Fund or make a financial order against them if they went ahead with making grants to parents of children who had not been physically injured that day, and the Trustees were forced to abandon these payments.

Although the Davies Report had found that the NCB's liability was "incontestable and uncontested" and it was widely felt that the NCB should have to bear the entire cost of removing the dangerous tips above Aberfan, Robens refused to pay the full cost, thereby putting the Trustees of the Disaster Fund under "intolerable pressure". Robens then "raided" the Fund for £150,000 to cover the cost of removing the tips – an action that was "unquestionably unlawful" under charity law – and the charity Commission took no action to protect the Fund from Robens's dubious appropriation of funds.

An important part of this fund is still alive and running. The Disaster Committee set up a fund to help students. This means that the output of the Committee's efforts is still available for students from the village or for children whose parents were living in Aberfan at the time of the disaster.

Spelbrook Memorial Woodland

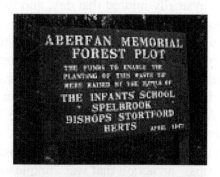

Shortly after the disaster children and staff at the primary school at spellbrook, near bishops Stortford, Hertfordshire, collected £20 16s for trees to be planted on a nearby tip. The forest plantation remains to this day.

Legislation

As a result of the concerns raised by the Aberfan disaster, and in line with Finding XVII of the Davies Report, in 1969 the British government framed new legislation to remedy the absence of laws and regulations governing mine and quarry waste tips and spoil heaps. The mines and Quarries (Tips) Act 1969. Was designed "to make further

106

provision in relation to tips associated with mines and quarries; to prevent disused tips constituting a danger to members of the public; and for purposes connected with those matters".

The new Act was an extension of the earlier Mines and Quarries Act 1954. As the Davies Tribunal had found, this Act did not mention tips at all in its provisions – in fact, the only reference to public safety in that Act was a section dealing with fencing abandoned or disused mines and quarries to prevent people falling into them. Moreover, under the terms of the 1954 Act, the Aberfan disaster was not even required to be formally reported to HN Inspectorate of mines and Quarries because it did not take place on colliery property and no mine workers had been injured or killed.

Heroes whose lives will never be the same

CHILDREN, COME UNTO ME

Children and teachers of Aberfan I pray for you
So many young lives cut short
Why was that mound not sorted?
Only now when it's too late
Did the company action take?
Aberfan a nation shares your grief
When a mountain moved
Destroying much beneath
Children starting the school day
As they sat and prayed
Not knowing that the mounting would move
Then a rumble like never before
As the mountain woke and gave a roar
Taking all in its path
Then came the aftermath
As the news began to spread
To the school many sped
The Rhondda united in grief
While they dig beneath
Listening for the faintest sound
Of those trapped beneath this mound
Aberfan still today for you I pray
Knowing that in Heaven the children play

Miners' Strike 1972, 1974 and 1984

On 9 January 1972 the British miners went on strike for the first time since 1926. The strike lasted for seven weeks and 135 pits closed in south Wales. A state of emergency was declared and to economize on electricity Edward Heath's government had to reduce the working week to three days. As a result of the strike, the miners' wages were increased, becoming among the highest among the British working class.

By 4 February 1974 the miners' situation had deteriorated and a national miners strike was called again. This strike lasted four weeks. A state of emergency and a three-day working week were once again declared. The Prime Minister, Edward Heath, called a General Election hoping that the electorate would support the Government's attempts to deal with the deteriorating industrial situation, but the Conservative Party was defeated. The new Labour government reached a deal with the miners shortly afterwards.

By 1984 the coal industry was in decline and the National Coal Board wished to close 20 pits, a situation that would have led to 20,000 men losing their jobs. The National Coal Board claimed that the contract made with the unions in 1974 was no longer valid because of the changes that had occurred in the British economy.

The Conservative Government, under Margaret Thatcher, was determined to diminish the power and influence of the Unions. The Unions themselves argued that the Government's policies were having a damaging effect on the coal communities.

WALES CONGRESS
In support of Mining Communities

WHEN THEY CLOSE A PIT

THEY KILL A COMMUNITY

STOP THEM! SUPPORT THE MINERS

Arthur Scargill, President of the National Union of Mineworkers (NUM), called on the miners to strike, and on 12 March a strike started which was to last for nearly a year. Miners from 28 south Wales pits played an influential role during the strike through their picketing and protesting.

Many movements were set up in support of the miners, such as Women against Pit Closures (WAPC). These women played an important role in the strike by raising money to help support the miners and their families.

Eventually the miners acknowledged defeat and returned to work on 5 March 1985 after calling the strike off two days earlier at a special NUM Conference. The coal industry continued to decline in south Wales with 12 pits closing within a year of the strike coming to an end.

Poems

The Bench

There is a bench in the Rhondda that I saw on my last visit
Today I was meditating and visualized myself on that bench
this is what came to me

Take a seat I'd like to show you a few things
Sit and be still you will be amazed at what you see
Mountains that are so high
Birds that fly in the sky
So many different shades go green
I've only seen before in my dreams
The sounds of children playing
As I remember some of you old sayings
This is the Rhondda in all its glory
I can tell you so many stories
Take my hand we'll fly over this land
And back at this bench we will land
Like the clouds soaring by
It's time that I say goodbye
I was truly blessed for I saw the Rhondda at its best
With a man who was above the rest
Yes my father took my hand
And showed me this glorious land

Miners Dig for Coal
As miners we dig for coal
In this dark and dusty hole
Cages we would cram in
Down the shaft to make a living
Flat we would lay paving the way
Placing dynamite
We blast all day and night
With just the beam of my lamb light
Moving tons of coal each fall
Making sure there's enough for all
When my shift ends
I'll have some stories to tell my friends

Sunrise over the Valley
Sunrise over the valley signals a new day
I promise to stop and listen to what others have to say
For life is not just about me it's about all of us
Brother and sisters we all are
Love for the valley I have by far
A place where we thrive there's no need to hide
Just stop and look around
We have mountains tall and grand
Rivers and streams that flow on by
A welcoming sight for sore eyes
The trees in many shades of green
Was for a long time in the valley never seen
Yes the scars are still there that's the price we have to bare
For this was a valley that we mined for coal
If only they could see when they closed the mines

We really didn't mind the work was hard and at a high price
At least there will be no more loss of life
I ask you today don't walk on by
Listen to others it may make you cry
But at least you are still alive

Dedicated to the memory of all Rhondda Valley miners

A Miners Son
A miner's son I'm proud to be
I can only imagine to see
The hardship my father went through
You can go down the pits today
Never will you see how it was in our yesterdays
At nineteen my father had to retire from the mines
With an illness miners call dust
Lungs beginning to decay each and everyday
Shortness of breath a chesty cough that is a miner's lot
Moving away from the Valley and hills
Prevented me suffering the same ills
I thanked my Dad for that as next to him I sat
Listening to tales of horror
Sadly my Dad won't have too many more tomorrows

This fills my heart with sorrow
The nurse said its time to say goodbye
Tears flowing from my eyes
Rest now Dad as I hold your hand
I will always remember wales is my Fathers Land
A miner's son I'm proud to be
I still feel my father close to me

126

The Cage

The clatter of the cage that takes me underground
My day begins on the pit face a cold and dark place
How far will we dig today no one can really say
They say we have targets to meet let's hope there's no gas
leaks
Pick axe and shovel in my hand I start to dig coal for this
land
With our output low or slow this mine they will close
People say we must be mad but in my heart I'm really glad
As I ascend for the last time from this dark dusty mine
I know for me tomorrow the sun will shine
On the welfare I'll have to sign because there is no more
mines
Men queuing for hours a day willing to work for little pay
For miners we are a band of brothers better than no other
A new trade we're willing to learn just for the chance to earn
Please don't let this valley die it is my life I cannot lie

Ferndale Colliery

As I Wake

I wake in the Rhondda Valley
With mountains so grand
If only people knew
The hardship under ground
A warren of tunnels
Where men work
Up to the top they come back
Their skin covered in black
The mountains may look so grand
Please spare a thought for those under ground

Days Of 74

I remember the days back in 74 when miners and
government went to war
Striking for what is right the government prolonged the fight
Turning father against son friend against friend
When all the miners wanted was this strike to end
A 3 day working week was brought in
Power cuts at night I remember sitting in candle light
All the miners wanted was fair pay
The government wouldn't let them have their say
Sadly the union gave in and the miner's working day begins
This was the start of the end for mining was coming to an
end
Soon the pit would lay silent many left for lent
Hanging up their tools for the last time
Leaving only memories of the mines
Men now struggling to find work bearing the scars of their

mining hurt
The valley is now silent but we are not sad
For there will be a better life for my lad
Some would never work again but they had earned the rest
from the pain
I remember the days of 74 they will live with me for
evermore

FERNDALE STRAND c1930s

Home to the Rhondda
I went home to the Rhondda today
Sarah and I had a lot to say
Sat on the bench taking in the view
Sarah it was nice to see you
Shane and Sadie not feeling too well
Love to be you hope you're soon well
Mountains so grand all around
It's lovely to listen to all the sounds
I'm sure your agree it's a magical place to go
I dedicated this poem
To Sarah Phillips

pantyffynnon colliery

Awake before the Lark

It's early I wake before the lark
I head up to the pit shaft that is so dark
My Buttys behind me we all sing our song
To carry our heavy tools we have to be strong
The first cage is full soon at speed we'll soon go down
To the dark dusty tunnels underground
For the next twelve hours these mines are ours
The first blast of the day as we start to earn our pay
My Davy lamp is my best friend until this dirty shifts ends
The whistle blows it's time to go back to the shaft we all
know
Cage by cage we come back up we can't wait to reach the

133

top

The doors flung open out we walk our song now turned to talk

Bones are aching our body's hurt to top it all we're spitting dirt

I know no other job so tomorrow I'll go back down to earn a few bob

Means So Much to Me

The Rhondda Valley means so much to me
It's where my Father used to be
Dinas born and bred mining to earn his bread
Thomas Pattimore was his name
Mining for a living caused him so much pain
At nineteen he was too ill for the mines
Lungs that were shot the dust had done its lot
Taking it slow he never complained
Short of breath for the rest of his life
Thank God he had a loving wife
It brought me to tears as the years went by
For I knew it won't be long before we say goodbye

The kindest man I had ever known
I'm proud to call the Rhondda my home

Sheep roam on the road
Mountains scared by coal
The narrow streets
With hills so steep
Chimneys pouring out smoke
It's enough to make you choke
This is the Rhondda in all its glory
The mines hold some horror stories
This is the Rhondda that I knew
The place where I mostly grew
Mine shafts now fallen silent
No more shall we dig coal
What shall become of the valley?
Sheep no longer roam the road

137

They have grass pens and feel at home
Mountains lush and green
Makes a lovely scene
The Rhondda become a beautiful place
Let's not forget those who worked on the pit face

St. Tanwg's Church, Llandanwg

My valley of green

How I miss my valley of green
Where still I remember my childhood dreams
The river in Dinas I would play
Climbing the mountains on sunny days
Sitting at the side of the track
Listening to the train go clickerty clack
Where the sheep would roam free
Following my brother and me
Up to Porth and Pandy
Where we had family
I remember my valley so green
And cherish the memories in my dreams

As A Child
As a child to my father I said
When I grow old a miner I want to be

He said son come with me
There's a sight I want you to see
Taking off his top I suddenly stopped
A body blackened by scars
Skin rough and hard
Then we sat by the fire side
With Dad giving a great big sigh
Picking up some coal dust
Saying is this what you lust
Breathe this in soon your done
For your lungs will be done
When you have your daily bath
The colour in your skin will last
Please son there's better than this
I tell you now mining I will not miss
Then to the cemetery we went next
Reading the headstones so many names
See son Mining is real it's not a game
The light of day these poor souls will never see again
Please son promise me this
Mining you will give a miss

The Carriage

As I hear the carriage coming down the track
Something wrong it's going to fast
Then suddenly a flash and blast
Blown clean of my feet
I landed about fifty feet
When the dust settled
All I could see was twist metal
There's my lamp with a dim glow
Laying below a ton of coal
Fist I check myself down
As I get up off the ground
In the darkness I look around
Then I hear my Butty groan
He'd taken the full blast
Body covered in splinters from the blast
Lay still my Butty they know we're here
Then we heard a tapping and shout
Listen Butty they are getting us out
I'm not going to make it my Butty said
As in my arms he laid his head
Rescuers break through the coal
Sadly their rescue was to slow
Dam this job of digging for coal

The Sign of a Miner

Blue scars darkened by coal
Run down the body for all to see
Caused by digging the coal seam
Your never hear a miner complain
As he loads the trucks of the coal train
The pain in their faces tells it all
Sights of horrors we've never seen
Life is hard when digging for coal
I cringed at the stories my dad told
The mines I never was destined to be
A better life my dad made for me
I'll never forget what my father did
All the time the pain he hid
Thank you Dad and Uncles too
This poem is dedicated to you

Church of our lady of Penrhys (Ferndale, Rhondda)

The Catholic church at Ferndale in the Rhondda.

It's full title is "church of our Lady of Penrhys" and it was built as a memorial to the original statue of Mary that until 1538 stood a few miles away in the town of Penrhys.

Legend has it that the Penrhys statue appeared in an oak tree and could not be removed by "even eight oxen" until the original shrine there was built for it but Henry VIII had the shrine burnt to the ground and the statue publically destroyed in London along with other religious artifacts as part of his dissolution of the monasteries.

A replica of the Penrhys statue is still housed in the church and another, larger than the original, now stands at the shrine site in Penrhys.

146

These photos of Porth are thought to have been taken 40 years a go

149

151

7569. SALEM CHAPEL, PORTH

7572. CYMMER COLLIERY

7573. LEWIS MERTHYR COLLIERY, HAFOD

154

My Father was a Miner.

My father was a miner, Of this I'm very proud ;
Working hard every day for such little pay . He worked so
far below the ground, where digging was the only sound. He
worked so hard with all his butts hoping each day their luck
would last. He crawled upon his belly. In tunnels so low and
narrow, the dust would on his lungs would leave a shadow.
He ate his food from a Tommy box, just a couple of slices of
bread, while squatting upon the ground, spitting dust with
bits of bread. Drinking water to wash down the dust that lay
in his throat. And in his lungs where it formed a deadly
crust. I'd wait on the doorstep I'd hear the clatter of his boots
, Then my dad came into sight : Along with a band of
brothers , my Dad, as black as black, His bath was always
ready, Set down in front of fire, I would then wash his back.
Right down his back blue scars and grime, but you cannot
wash away scars from the mine Years now have passed
since he worked the mines but I am proud to say,
MY FATHER WAS A MINER, BUT SADLY HAS
NOW PASSED AWAY

Tears

Tears I have to hide away
Words I cannot find to say
I have to be strong in front of others
When on my own the tears flow
As I make sense why you had to go
I will always remember your smiling face
And my life how you graced
You came into my life when I was low
You thought me all there is to know
Now I can make it on my own
It was time for you to go

It's 5am time for me to rise
I climb out of bed blurry eyed
Creeping round the house
Being quite as a mouse

My good lady wakes with me
To do my lunchbox and cup of tea
My shift starts at seven
It not a job made in heaven

For down the pit I will go
For twelve hours my lamp will glow
Pulling on my mining gear
For time is drawing near

As I leave my house
I'll join my Butty's
We sing our miners song
As we march along

An hour seems like three
As we work on bended knees
With the drill in my hand
At the coal I start to pound

When my shift is done
How much more damage to my lungs
My spit is black as coal
In my lungs it will burn a hole

But I'll carry on you see

Because I'm a miner that's just me
I live each day as if it's my last
For it only takes one big blast

My family won't see me again
As I'm trapped in this den
I may be buried so deep
This mine my body will keep

As my soul is set free
No more mining for me
I'm now in Heaven no more
dust
My love for my family will always last

My Little Carney

Little carney sing your song
All my shift long I'll whistle to you
As long as we see this shift through
If I don't hear your song
I know I may not have long
Retreat I must for one spark could ignite this dust
You gave your life to save me
Now you sing your song in heavens trees

My dad was a miner in the Rhondda
It shortened his life he could live no longer
Chewing dust each day swilling water to wash it away
My dad would sing on the way to the mines
Not knowing if this was to be the last time
I'm proud of my father and his mining days
I just wish that for longer he could have stayed
I love you dad just like the old days
Every night for you I kneel and pray
I look after mum like I promised to do
Her heart every day is broken for you
I ask God to keep you safe
Now you're both in your final resting place
Your mining memorabilia I still have today
I keep it in the cabinet on display
I'm proud of you dad more than I can say
I love you even more than yesterday

The Rhondda

I thought of the Rhondda today
Where in the good old days I used to play
Play on the mountains and in the parks
Staying out in the street till it got dark
Everyone knowing each other
Friends were more like sister and brother
Never needing doors to be locked
Neighbors just gave a gentle knock
A community I've never know better
When people used to write letters
Looking out for each other
Everyone known as Aunty or Uncle
Mining history on every mantle
I'm honored to have shared this period in time
When everyone's dad worked down the mines
It made me what I am today
I'd give anything to relive those days

A book you must write
To tell of the miners plight
A valley steeped in so much pain
As underground they dig the coal vain
Heroes of the day working for little pay
The hardship that was endured
Today it would never be heard
A happy band of men
Every family were friends
So a book you will write
To put all the stories right

This was given me by my spirt guide
White Bear

My valley was so green before the coal and dust
Survival was a must and digging for that black gold dust
The forests on the mountain side slowly disappeared
Taking away the beauty we had for years
Props made for underground to keep our miners safe and
sound
Digging a shaft up to a mile below sometimes the going was
slow
Starting to tunnel when they hit the coal its hell working in
this hole
I'll never complain for I have a job, due its hard is a miner's
lot
When that coal seam comes to an end the hand I'll shake of
my friends
A new pit we must start due I must like working in this dark
An explosion shakes the ground then all is silent all around.
Collect my thoughts put into action what I was thought
Check around listen for the slightest sound
Why the hell did I come underground?
My Buttys are all safe now how to get out of this place
Shifting the rubble slowly checking each move
Hush now lads did you hear that sound
We will soon be back above ground

My Grandfather Will Gregson worked in Cwmparc colliery all his life from a very early age to retirement..... we never knew him to have lost a day's work ever....The only time that he was away from the pit, was during his war service, where her was injured by bomb shrapnel, losing his left arm, and the top of his skull...and had a silver plate there....to look at him you never know was beneath that bald head... When he returned home, he immediately went back to work in the pit! He was a REAL man...as most men were in those days.... Unfortunately, three months after he retired....he simply lay down.... and passed away...I'll never Forget you Pop....I miss you to this very day!

Ken Gregson has kindly let me share this reply to a poem I put on Rhondda our valley
Thank you Ken
My dad was a miner poem

Herbert Street Treherbert holds a place in my heart
It's where my dream really did start
Sat on the bench watching children play
It makes you smile when you hear what they say
Watching the mountains with the morning mist
Is a sight surely you must not miss
Looking at PenPych a mountain so high
The top of it disappears in the sky
The bench is a special place
Where I train the mind not to race
With family living close by
It's always hard to say goodbye
Sarah, Neil, Shane and Sadie to
You all inspire me to do what I do
In the New Year I will return
To sit on that bench I yearn

A verse from Ray Jones who lived in Blaenrhondda until the fire in the 60s

Hi Brian,

I lived in Caroline Street in Blaenrhondda until the fire in 1960,

And I have always remembered this verse that we sang there as youngsters.

We are the Caroline boys
We never make a noise
We mind our manners
And spend our tanners
For we are the Caroline boys.

Tonight I'll sit and say a prayer
For all those lives that was not spared
They gave their lives so we shall live
No greater sacrifice they could give
Now with the Angels you sleep   Your memory I promise to
keep   Sleep tight my friend I never knew My respect lies
with you

Dad

Dad can I go down the mines
To carry on the family line
No my son was the reply   With a tear in my father eye
What shall I do for work I had to ask?
Dad held me in a gentle clasp
Son I want your life to last
Not working with that dangerous blast
Dad mining is in my soul
It is my only goal
With a cough and spit
Dad showed me the true pit
What shall I do for work I asked again?
If only I could take away your pain
Son you stay above ground
Whatever you do you and I are sound

Oh Rhondda how beautiful you are
Since the healing of mining scars
Father and son at last can go to work
Knowing there's no risk of hurt
The mountains turned from black to green   Where once the
slag heaps could be seen   My heart filled with pride   As the
sun shines on the mountain side To think my father once
worked underground   Of this lush green land   The
Rhondda continues to grow   It's memories I cannot let go
All those who worked down the mines   My respect for you
is divine   Now the grey has turned to green   Vibrant
colours so long not seen   How green was my Valley we
used to say   During those mining days   Now the trees and
green return   My Valley for you I yearn

Treherbert

Corbett Street is a tiny place

Where I could sit and meditate   So many views to see   I feel my mother close to me   A Row of houses with mountains behind Is the perfect place to calm the mind   In ore was my first sight   I wait to see the stars at night   So Corbett street the place to be   Where my family draw close to me

Llwynypia, the unveiling of the statue to Archibald Hood - mine owner

Rhondda Valleys, Llwynypia, Gelligaled Baths

Llwynypia, Partridge Road

Treherbert Rail Station

Treherbert - Penpych from Bute Street

Fernhill Colliery Treherbert.

Treherbert, Fernhill Colliery

Treherbert Reservoir

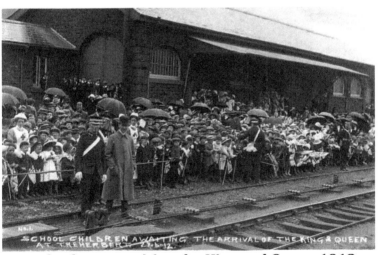

Treherbert - awaiting the King and Queen 1912

Treorchy High St 1910's

Treorchy - the Gorsedd Circle

Pontygwaith, Llewellyn Street

Porth Colliery 1931

Porth Carnival 1910

Tylorstown, Queens Square and Tram 1900's

Stanleytown, General View

Tonypandy General View

Tonypandy Nant Gwyn Colliery 1927

Trehafod - Rhondda Heritage Park - once the Lewis Merthyr Colliery

Trehafod, Trehafod Road circa 1910's

Trealaw, Brithweunydd Road 1940's

Clydach Vale and Upper Tonypandy

A view of Blaenllechau

The owner of the Glamorgan Coal Mines - Archibald Hood - was much admired by the community, and on his passing they erected a statue in his honor.

Llwynypia hospital was where many of the children of the Rhondda Valleys were born in the 20th century.

Rhondda Valleys, Llwynypia Colliery (Coal Mine)

Llwynypia and Tonypandy from Penrhys

Treherbert Hospital 1930's

Treherbert - a view from the Rhigos

Treorchy, Wynne's Garages Ltd. of Ynyswen Road

Pentre High School

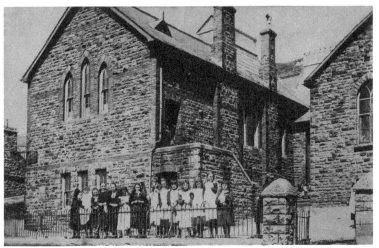

Pentre Higher Grade School and Pupils in 1902

Pentre, Great Landslide - October 1916

General View, Pentre, Rhondda

Pentre - General View

Pentre - Llewellyn Street

Blaenrhondda General View

189

Trealaw Brass Band 1890

The Salisbury Hotel - now the Ferndale Rugby

Club The Salisbury Hotel in Blaenllechau - above - was once run by my great grandfather - Edward Evans - who then moved on to own the White Rock Hotel in Penygraig.

Clydach Vale, Adams Street Floods

Blaenclydach, Clydach Road 1905

Clydach, Cambrian Colliery 1900

Cymmer Colliery

Rhondda Valleys, Dinas Railway Station 1954

Dinas has the distinct 'honor' of being the place where the first deep mine was sunk in the Rhondda Valleys in 1812. In 1806 at Dinas - just a short distance away from Porth - Walter Coffin leased the rights to minerals under several farms. His venture was successful, and he soon built a roadway from Dinas to Gyfeillion (Hopkinstown). From there the coal was taken on to Treforest where it was hauled to its destination by canal.

After that more coal mines in the Rhondda Valleys were opening at the rate of several a year. It was almost inevitable then that disaster would eventually strike, and in 1856 at nearby Cymmer Colliery the earth trembled thunderously as the first major explosion took place in a local Colliery (Coal Mine). 114 men and boys lost their lives that day. It was the first major disaster at a Rhondda Colliery, leaving widows and mothers weeping the length and breadth of the Valleys. It would not be the last.

At the top of the Rhondda Fach are Ferndale and ultimately Maerdy. Maerdy will always have a special place in the Rhondda's history books as the location of the last coal mine in the Rhondda Valleys.

FERNDALE.

THE LIBRARY, GELLI YSTRAD.

Hopkinstown is the first village in the Rhondda Valleys after leaving Pontypridd. It boasts the Chapel - Capel Rhondda - where the Cwm Rhondda was first sung. To

Penrhys is the site of what was once one of the holiest places in Wales. It was the site of a Cistercian Abbey, a holy well, and a statue described as beauty beyond belief. All that now remains at Penrhys is the holy well of St Mary, and a replacement (1953) statue of Mary and Jesus. It is probable that the well pre-dates Christianity. Much of what once stood at Penrhys was of course destroyed during the Reformation period. Pilgrims still travel to this medieval holy place from far and wide

Penygraig, White Rock Hotel

The History of the Rhondda Valleys.

Before coal was mined in the area known then as Ystradyfodwg - later to become known as the Rhondda Valleys - the area was amongst the most picturesque in Wales. It was described by Charles Cliffes as having "meadows of emerald greenness", and the air as being "aromatic with the scent of wild flowers and mountain plants"

By the time the area became known as the Rhondda Valleys, the description would have dramatically changed, and few places in the Valleys had escaped the blackness from the coal dust that spread through the Rhondda Rivers and covered the Rhondda Mountains with coal waste.

The overwhelming majority of the Rhondda Valleys households where occupied by colliers and their families, and certainly in the

Early days trades associated with house building, as all of the thousands of Rhondda terraced houses were new builds. The stone for these houses was quarried from the hillsides where the houses were being built, and can still be seen today

The houses were very basic, with stone slab floors downstairs, no electricity, and a small toilet (Ty Bach) at the bottom of the garden. The cooking facilities at the time were a cast iron range with a coal fire center and cast iron ovens each side. A kettle to boil water could either be suspended above the fire or rested directly on the fire. Rhondda folk would often be seen holding a piece of bread in front of the fire making toast. Lighting was by oil lamps and/or candles, until later when gas was installed and most rooms had a gas light, and the kitchen had a four ringed stove with a two tier oven. To take a bath hot water was poured into a large tin bath which had been placed near the front of the fire.

The Chapel played a big part in the lives of the early Rhondda dwellers, and most people would have attended regularly in their local village or town, which would have had a choice of several.

Many Rhondda women died during childbirth, which certainly in the early days would be in their own homes. Even if mother and baby survived childbirth, child mortality was high due to their living conditions, poor diets, and the many diseases that were prevalent in those days.

Because many were widowed either by accidents at the mines or during childbirth, lots would have been married more than once. It was essential for a man to find a new wife to care for his surviving children, and for a woman to find a new husband to provide an income - there was no national assistance in those days.

So, the background of the Rhondda Valleys was one of hard work, poverty, bereavement, and in many cases short lives.

A close up of the much improved War Memorial in Porth, Rhondda Valleys

One of the most noticeable movements of recognizable landmarks during the building of the Rhondda by-pass was that of the War Memorial and Cenotaph in Porth. This was dismantled and re-assembled close by. The re-dedication and opening ceremony took place on Sunday the 6th May 2007.

Three Countries.
One Community.
Together then, now & always.
Remember the 1984 miners' strike...

The miners' strike was the beginning of the closure of the mines in the Rhondda and across the UK. This resulted in thousands of men being put on the Dole and communities suffered as a result. In the Rhondda the community was at first strong but as time went on and work harder to find many miners left the Rhondda in search of work many moving to London and the south coast. This splitting up families

Porthcawl

Porthcawl is one of the main seaside resorts that people from the Rhondda go to, I have many memories of Porthcawl from when I was a child up to 2014 when I last visited there to see my Cousin Carol Seals. Although Porthcawl has changed over the years it is nice to see that the sand dunes have survived with the funfair not as big as I remembered (but maybe it just looked bigger as a child) where I once had fun on the rides my Grandchildren now do the same

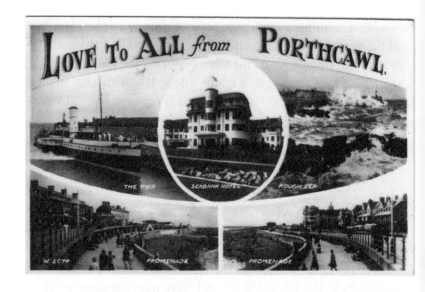

LOVE TO ALL from PORTHCAWL.

THE PIER   SEABANK HOTEL   ROUGH SEA

W 2074   PROMENADE   PROMENADE

Children's Paddling Pool, Porthcawl.